MAKING FAST ELECTRIC MODEL POWER BOATS

MAKING
FAST ELECTRIC
MODEL
POWER BOATS

IAN WILLIAMS

THE CROWOOD PRESS

First published in 2023 by
The Crowood Press Ltd
Ramsbury, Marlborough
Wiltshire SN8 2HR

enquiries@crowood.com

www.crowood.com

British Library Cataloguing-in-Publication Data
A catalogue record for this book is available from the British Library.

ISBN 978 0 7198 4259 7

Acknowledgements
First and foremost, I must thank my wife Norma for putting up with me during the writing of this book. It couldn't have been easy.
   I would also like to thank all the members of the Northern Amp Draggers, the MPBA Fast Electric Section and the guys at Bridlington MBS for their help and friendship. Special thanks go to Martin Marriott, Peter Barrow and Ian Phillips, as well as to Tony Ellis, of Model Marine Supplies. Last, but certainly not least, I would like to thank Walter Geens, the President of NAVIGA, for his help over the years.

Picture credits
Walter Geens, pages 19 (top), 25 (top right), 26 (top) and 108 (bottom left); Walter Geens and NAVIGA page 125 (top left); D Harvey, pages 8 (bottom), 9, 10 and 12 (bottom); Arne Hold page 130 (bottom); Rich Marsh, pages 133 (right top, middle and bottom) and p.135 (all); Bill Oxidean, page 97 (bottom right); James Smithson, page 17 (bottom); Wikimedia Commons page 6.

Typeset by Envisage IT

Cover design by Bluegecko

Printed and bound in India by Thomson Press India Ltd.

Contents

Chapter One

In the Beginning

Radio control (RC) was first demonstrated to the public in 1898 at the Madison Square Garden arena in New York City, by none other than the legendary inventor and engineer Nikola Tesla. The

The very first RC model: Nikola Tesla's 'Devil Automata' boat.

vehicle that Tesla had built for the demonstration – described as a 'teleautomaton' – was a model boat and, yes, it was electric! Tesla also referred to it as his 'Devil Automata', as he recognised early on its potential for use in remotely controlled weaponry.

As far as RC models are concerned, Tesla's ideas moved on and into World War I. Germany made use of radio control to send small, fast, explosive-filled boats to attack British warships. These were not very successful, however, and the same was more or less true of similar devices tried in World War II. In the years after the end of the war, a huge number of electronic components that had not been used by the Armed Forces became available very cheaply on the open market. Items such as relays, small motors, resistors and especially valves were put to good use by individuals with the necessary knowledge of radio, who began to experiment and make their own radio control equipment.

By the 1950s, a few commercially made systems began to be made available. In the USA, internal combustion (IC) models were beginning to appear, based on the full-sized hydroplanes that were being used for racing. The full-sized boats used ex-military Allison engines based on the Rolls Royce Merlin from the Mustang fighter planes and ran anti-clockwise around an oval course. There was a simple reason for this: as full-sized boats ran their props clockwise, when viewed from the stern, factors such as prop torque, and so on, meant that it was easier for the boats to turn left.

Internal diagram of Tesla's boat with all its various bits and bobs.

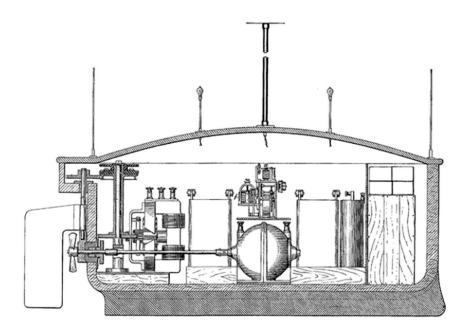

Model motors (including electric motors), on the other hand, generally rotate anti-clockwise when viewed from the shaft end of the motor. This means that models perform better when turning to the right. After a short while, it was decided to change the oval course for model racing to a clockwise one. Later, speed record events were

An early RC transmitter, probably dating from the mid- to late 1950s. Note the steering wheel.

Another 1950s transmitter, in a different, ship's-wheel style but still with the huge switches.

expanded to include a one-third mile oval and also a one-eighth mile (two times one-sixteenth) straightaway (SAWS).

In the mid- to late 1950s, radio equipment was improving and becoming more readily available commercially. Hull developments led to interesting increases in speeds, with the result that more people were drawn to the hobby. It was around this time that two young men who were to have a profound effect on RC boat racing appeared on the scene: Tom Perzentka and Ed Hughey. Tom founded Octura Models in 1954 and a little later Ed started Hughey Boats Inc. Octura became famous mainly for its props, but also produced hardware and boats, while Ed had his own line of hardware and boat designs. Both men did much to further the hobby. A little later Ed developed an interest in electric power, using some of the motors from the recently developing RC car scene. He designed and manufactured gearboxes for the new powerful brushed motors and electric boat speed started to increase significantly. In the 1990s I was the importer of Hughey Boats products into the UK and part of Europe, and during that time Ed Hughey taught me almost everything I know about fast electric (FE) boats.

The development of FE boats in the UK and Europe was different from that in the USA. Although the development of RC proceeded pretty much in the same way as it had in the USA, using ex-military discards, in the UK the focus in FE tended to be on submerged-drive boats. The Model Power Boat Association (MPBA) was formed in 1924 and events were soon being organised, mainly for IC boats. As in the USA, the progress in the design and function in both RC and hull design increased boat speeds. In the late 1950s, people were starting to use electric powered boats, but these were mainly of the MTB (motor torpedo boat) and fast launch types. The boats were often to scale and used for steering type speed competitions. With the formation of NAVIGA in 1958, the world-wide organisation concerned with model ship building and model ship sport, originally with

The underside of the 1960s F1 boat showing the wire drive and small rudder. Note also the hull shape and how thin the moulding is.

F1E boat from the 1960s, with silver zinc cells. At the rear of the boat are the steering servo and above that a servo fitted with two micro-switches for series/ parallel battery switching.

A homemade charger for silver zinc cells. The charging current was only in milliamps.

A Ripmax Orbit motor that was used in the 100-watt class.

only three countries (not including the UK), the situation began to get really interesting. Although there had been significant developments in the USA in the period between the late 1940s and the late 1950s and early 1960s, as far as FE boats are concerned, it was in the 1960s when activity really started to pick up. Competitions began to have formalised classes and RC became more sophisticated, allowing several boats to be run at the same time in 'multi-racing' events.

The UK later became a member of NAVIGA probably around 1965. The organisation's events were run on three courses, two of which were used for FE racing as well as IC: F1E speed, F2 (a scale boat steering course) and F3E steering. In F1E, boats undertook a time run of the three 30-metre sides of a triangle once in each direction, with a 180-degree turn mid-way along the base of the triangle. The boat with the quickest time was the winner of the competition. A great test of skill, F3E involved steering around and through pairs of buoys set out in a

Some brushed competition motors from the 1960s: (left to right) three of Dereck Holder's homemade motors. The first was one of his original 1kg motors; the second is the final version with the 1mm prop shaft grub screwed directly into the motor shaft to save weight; the third is of the final +1kg motor again with a 2mm shaft grub screwed directly into the motor shaft, the fourth is a Keller motor made in Germany. All these motors ran on 42 volts.

triangle shape, with the fastest clear round winning. (*See* Chapter 13 for more on these courses.)

F1E was split into 30-watt, 100-watt and 500-watt classes. The boats were not fast by today's standards. *Marksman* was a 100-watt boat probably designed by Philip Connolly back in the 1960s, using silver zinc cells. It may not have been an out-and-out competition boat, but its speeds were quoted as 10 to 12mph. The rather odd-looking *Moccasin* was on a par in terms of performance.

Although F3E and F1E are still on the NAVIGA competition list, they are not run in the UK today, as interest in these particular classes seems to have died out.

Much development has been undertaken between then and now. It would really need a whole book on its own to trace every single increase in design and performance, but there are four major

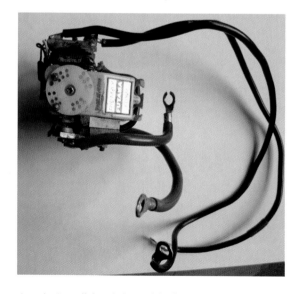

A series/parallel switcher with silver contacts, mounted on a servo.

developments that have led to the latest very fast models. Apart from advances in hull design, which are still ongoing, cell technology and improvements in motors have been the main factors. The first significant boost to performance was the arrival of the NiCad cell, followed by the NimH cell. Second was the development of high-power modified brushed motors. The last two huge improvements were the introduction of the brushless motor and LiPo cells. This rather simplistic explanation brings the technology up to where it is today. It is also worth recognising that the development of electric flight and RC cars has also been a great provider of technology for the FE boating world.

Fellow competitors in the Northern Amp Draggers club and at national level have been generous with descriptions and photos from the early years of the sport. One of these is David Harvey, who as a young man in the 1960s raced at international level. When David and his brother

Internal view of an early 1960s 100-watt boat, Marksman, *designed by Phillip Connolly. Although it was not known as an out-and-out competition boat, it was reputed to do around 12mph.*

Another view of Marksman.

Marksman at speed. It appears as this was probably around its maximum speed of 10–12mph.

Moccasin, *an unusual design from the early 1960s. It seems to have two lead acid batteries fitted, probably 6-volt motorcycle types.*

Martin first went into fast electrics in the 1960s the classes were 30-watt, 100-watt and 500-watt. The cell for the 30-watt was a small square flat unit, but silver zinc cells were used for the bigger classes. In the 30-watt class the Russians used salt cells. However, it was discovered that the first attempt served to warm the cells up, while on the second attempt they had more than 30 watts, so the cells were eventually banned. In those days competitors had five minutes to get two attempts at the course, but if they missed a buoy at the first attempt, they were not allowed to try for a second go. The current rules allow five minutes to get in as many attempts as possible.

In the 1960s the boats varied in size from one not much bigger than a large hand to big versions that had to be lifted into the water by two people. In the 1970s, the classes changed to 1kg and +1kg, but now the classes have changed again to just one class – F1E – because it was found that competitors were adding just a little extra weight in a 1kg boat and then running it in the +1kg class.

A group of competitors in the +1kg class at the European Championships at Kiev (Kyiv) in the 1960s: (left to right) Dereck Holder 1st place, David Harvey 2nd, and 'Zander' 3rd. In front is the junior champion, Dereck's son Daniel.

Chapter Two

Hull Types and Design Considerations

The hull is one of the most important elements to consider when constructing a model boat. No matter how good and expensive the equipment in a boat, if the hull is not up to scratch, it will probably all be a waste of time and money. A little knowledge of what it all means and what to look out for is a good idea.

THE BASICS

There are really only two basic hull types for boats: displacement and planing. Although in the modern full-sized world the two types can interact and overlap, in the world of fast electric-powered RC boats, the planing type is more relevant. There are many variations of the basic planing hull type, both full size and model size, and it is wise to avoid becoming bogged down in theory and details of design. However, it is useful to have an understanding of the basics of both full-size and model hulls and of the most important variations, and to be aware of the difference each can make. Those who wish to immerse themselves in theory will find many photographs and diagrams online, along with massive amounts of information, especially from builders of full-size boats.

(Note: some of the photographs in this chapter are used to illustrate a particular point, but may incorporate other features that are not discussed here. In that case, they will be covered later, in the relevant chapter.)

HULL DESIGN

A brief explanation of how a displacement hull pushes through the water can help in understanding how a planing hull works. The classic image of a full-size ship at sea shows a typical wave formation. As the hull is powered through the water, it will push the water ahead of it, causing a bow wave to form. At the same time, it pushes water sideways and down. This downward movement will cause a wave formation known as a stern wave. A displacement hull will ride between the bow wave and the stern wave. As the speed increases, the hull will try to get over the 'hump' of the bow wave, which is not a good effect with this type of hull. The water will not be able to react quickly enough and the stern wave will fall astern of the hull. With diminishing support at the stern, the bow will lift, the bow wave will get bigger, and the hull will tend to ride on the down slope of the rear side of the bow wave. This could be a dangerous position as the hull will more than likely become unstable.

Despite the disadvantages of the displacement hull, it is possible for this type of structure to be really fast. One prime example is the World War II German *Schnellboot* (or E-Boat), which could do around 50mph, but this was a very specific hull design and had a lot of power!

This basic explanation of displacement hulls should help with an understanding of the concept of the planing hull. The planing hull is designed to

It is said that a flat plate is the most efficient planing form. This model seems to prove it, but turning may be less straightforward.

make use of the hydrodynamic lift caused by the forward motion, allowing the hull to lift itself over the bow wave and rise up in the water, thus reducing drag. This also reduces wave making and tends to stabilise the hull. To expand on this explanation, a fast boat achieves high speeds by dragging itself out of the water and skimming or planing over the surface, using hydrodynamic lift (the pressure of water on the bottom of the boat) to support its weight. Only by coming out of the water and drastically reducing wetted area can high speeds be attained without the need for huge amounts of power.

In theory, the best planing surface is a flat plate, but in practice this would be totally unusable. There would be no space for accommodation, motors and so on, and the boat would be unable to turn without major stability problems. If, however, a flat plate is bent down its centre line at an angle of 20 degrees or so, the basic V-shaped hull bottom starts to become apparent. Add a bow shape for non-planing operation, some sides to give the hull volume, a deck and a transom, and the basic V hull appears. Obviously, it is not as simple as that in real

A displacement hull at normal operating speed.

An overpowered displacement hull. The hull is trying to push over the bow wave and the stern is not being supported, resulting in a dangerous situation.

life. Such things as structural integrity, machinery space, accommodation and so on, are all factors, not to mention that the hull has to be as smooth-riding as possible for the sake of the humans inside it. Of course, with a fast model boat, there is no need to worry about crew comfort or injury caused by a rough ride, as long as there is room in the hull for motor, batteries and RC gear. Model boats are relatively much stronger than full-sized ones and are less likely to be damaged by stresses to the hull.

In the main, the design of model boats has developed from that of the full-size versions (and sometimes the other way round), but there is one major factor that has caused model boat design to diverge from full-size practice, especially with out-and-out racing boats. That is the fact that it is not possible to scale water! While a small ripple of the surface might be nothing to a full-size boat, it could be the equivalent of a 2-foot wave to a model. In addition, there is no guarantee that even an exact scale replica of a very efficient and fast full-size boat will work in model form. In fact, the probability is that there would be various problems getting the hull working well at all, and it would be necessary to introduce modifications to make it perform even reasonably well. (Note that this refers to models of competition boats, not models of cabin cruisers, or other types.)

TERMINOLOGY: STRUCTURE

Various terms may need explaining at this point. For example, many people will know what a 'hard chine' hull looks like, but what does the term actually mean? Looking at the basic V hull, the angle of the hull bottom from the horizontal is known as the 'deadrise' angle and can determine how the hull behaves in rough water. With the addition of hull sides, the sharp change of angle at the junction between hull bottom and hull side is known as the 'chine line'. In boat building parlance, any sharp change of angle is termed 'hard', so we have the term 'hard chine'.

The distance between the waterline and the deck edge is called the 'freeboard'. Some full-size boats, which may have to cope with rough water at times but still require a high-speed performance, have a modified so-called 'soft chine' hull where the chine line has been curved slightly. This type of hull may also be found on some small sailing dinghies. Having a hard chine allowed water to be pushed sideways instead of just running backwards along the hull, giving the hull lift and reducing wetted area. Flat-bottomed and shallow V hulls tend to bounce and slam in the rough, whereas a deep-V hull with a deadrise angle of 20 degrees or more will carve its way through waves and will handle rough water much better.

The early deep-V hulls had a deadrise that ran for the entire length of the boat. Often called a 'monohedron' hull, this was found to work quite well in rough conditions but could lack stability. Designers trying to improve the all-weather capabilities came up with a 'modified-V' hull. This compromise gave the front of the hull a wedge shape to slice through the water but altered the wedge to a flatter angle as it moved towards the stern of the boat. This is often called a 'warped-bottom' hull.

As it became clear that some water would not be deflected by the chine and could run up the side of the hull, causing drag, further design developments introduced 'chine rails'. These are add-ons to the hull, where the bottom of the boat meets the sides. They serve to deflect spray, improve lift and turning response and offer greater stability.

As more experience was gained with small planing hulls, it was found necessary to fit external longitudinal strengthening strips to the bottom of the hull. The hull would actually ride on the area between pairs of these strips and be lifted more, often producing more speed. Consequently, the strips were developed to become an integral part of the design of the hull. Almost all fast boats today will feature one or more pairs of these 'spray rails' (sometimes referred to as 'lifting strakes'), which have been developed to deflect water downwards and away from the hull, both to generate lift and to minimise wetted area.

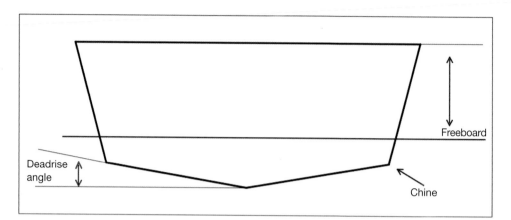

A basic planing hull shown at the transom, demonstrating the basic terms of reference.

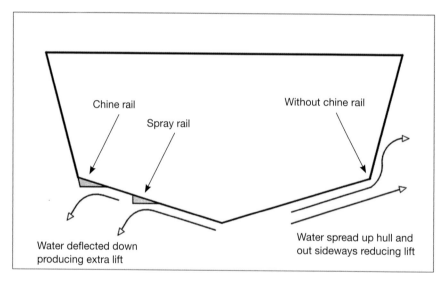

Planing hull showing the effect that chine rails and spray rails have on the lift component.

In the world of full-size powerboats there are constant design changes and tweaks to the basic planing hull structure, sometimes in pursuit of better performance, sometimes purely for the comfort of passengers. Of course, the same progress in design also applies to model boats, and the information given here can only be very basic. There are so many different ways of achieving the same effect with small design changes that a detailed description would take up most of this book, even if it were possible to track them all down. The information that follows will cover the types and classes of boat that are most common, any major differences from full-size hull design, and some features that would definitely not appear on a full-size boat.

FACTORS AFFECTING PERFORMANCE

Note: the information here refers almost exclusively to competition-type hulls. For more on scale-type hulls, *see* Chapter 14.

The first thing people (usually, but not always, young boys) ask at the lakeside is 'How fast is it?' If you know the answer, fine. If not, you can always explain the following and see if they are interested. The speed of a boat is directly governed by the following factors:

• the hull type;
• the power available from the motor;

- the weight of the boat;
- the efficiency of the drive system and propeller in converting the power of the motor into forward motion; and
- the amount of contact the hull has with the water.

As a boat that is designed to plane moves forward over or through the water, the effect of water flowing over the hull surface produces drag, due to viscosity and friction. Hydrodynamic drag is one of the major factors that affect performance, and the amount of drag a boat is subject to is directly proportional to its wetted area. Fortunately, within certain parameters (the law of diminishing returns applies), the faster a boat goes the greater the hydrodynamic lift. This means that the planing area required to support the boat's weight will decrease. The heavier a boat is, the more planing area it will need to support its weight, and the more drag it will be subject to.

Heavy boats have more inertia (resistance to acceleration) and will not accelerate as well from a standing start. Also, they may not handle or change direction as well as a light boat. A light boat will therefore almost always be faster than a heavier boat. It will also be more agile and easier to drive, except in rough water conditions where a heavier boat will have the advantage. Of course, model boat enthusiasts will invariably encounter 'disturbed' water, so they have a decision to make! This is all relative, of course. With the power that modern brushless motors provide, a few grams here or there will not make very much difference to performance. If a boat is overweight by 100 grams or so, however, that will be a different story!

MODERN HULL TYPES: SPORTS (FUN) AND COMPETITION

Monohulls

There are two subtypes of monohull: those that have the props and rudders in the water under the hull (submerged drive) and those that have the prop and rudder behind the transom (back) of the boat with a surface-piercing prop being used (surface drive).

Monohulls have a single hull and a single large planing area. Some designs incorporate one or more 'steps' in the hull bottom, although the norm appears to be a single step. In the UK and Europe, virtually all surface-drive racing monos are stepped, whilst submerged-drive boats are not. In the USA, generally, with one or two exceptions,

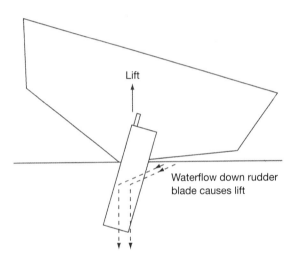

A rudder can significantly affect the handling of a heeled-over monohull in a turn.

A very different-looking Eco Expert boat from MHZ. It is unusual to see these boats with decals like this.

stepped hulls are banned from competition and straight keels are the norm, even with surface-drive boats.

Submerged Drive

Most submerged-drive monos are intended for so-called 'multi' racing and are a mixture of semi-flat-bottomed and shallow-V, usually with the V becoming much sharper towards the bow. Some have a shallow rounded hull with pronounced chine rails and quite often the hull will have no freeboard at all. In this case, the deck is angled down to the hull and in effect becomes the chine rail.

One of my early submerged-drive boats, with homemade wire drive and a curved hull bottom.

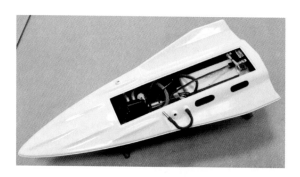

A Mini Eco class model: a modern submerged-drive race boat that runs anti-clockwise around a triangle course. This Type 2007 is a very competitive European boat.

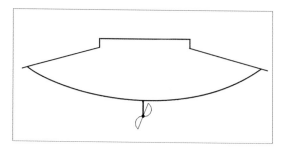

The hull on the submerged-drive boat has no deadrise, and the deck slopes down and overlaps the edge of the hull to form the chines.

The multi classes require boats with instant acceleration from rest and out of corners, and precise handling, with minimum speed loss during turning. Most multi boats are functional in appearance, bearing very little similarity to full-size craft. In Europe there are several submerged-drive classes, while in the UK there are only two classes on the books for national competition. These are Eco Expert and Mini Eco Expert. (For more on all the classes, *see* Chapter 13.)

Surface Drive

Surface-drive monohulls tend to have a semi-scale resemblance (although only a passing one) to full-size craft. While they can be much faster in a straight line, especially if the hull is stepped, the handling characteristics of a surface-drive mono fall short of a submerged-drive multi boat. In common with their full-size counterparts, model

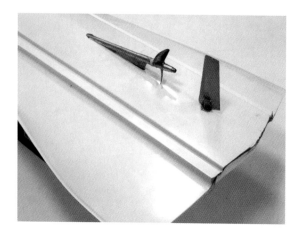

The underside of the Mini Eco boat, showing a narrow raised centre section, which is the boat's running surface.

An Eco Expert hull flat out in choppy water. Note the wire drive line and the fact that it has a parallel thrust line.

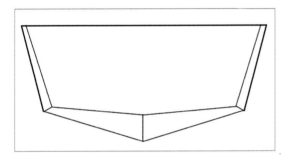

A modified-V or warped-bottom hull – note how the V reduces in angle towards the stern.

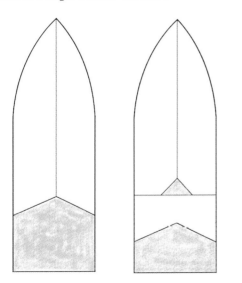

The 'footprints' of monohulls: a standard V hull on the left and a stepped hull to the right.

deep Vs do not like to turn very tightly at full speed. A stepped hull tends to run flatter in a turn with much less heel and can be made to turn quite effectively when correctly set up for oval racing.

Unstepped V hulls with surface drive have one drawback in comparison with other types of boat, and this is that they bank over when turning. This presents the rudder to the water at an angle, allowing it to generate lift when turning. This can cause the boat to wobble and hop around, and may result in it spinning. This can also happen with stepped hulls, although to a lesser degree.

Catamarans and Tunnel Hulls

Catamarans (usually referred to as cats) and tunnels are actually a development of the monohull and have two narrow hulls joined by a bridging section. Offshore cats invariably have surface drives and tunnels usually have outboard motors. They are generally more laterally stable and have less wetted area than a monohull. They also have the benefit of riding on the cushion of air trapped between the sponsons to partially support the weight of the boat and further reduce wetted area and drag.

There are a number of differences between a cat hull and a tunnel hull. Model tunnel hulls are usually semi-scale replicas of the full-size F1 racing boats and fitted with outboard motors. There are commercial kits available, but there are no official

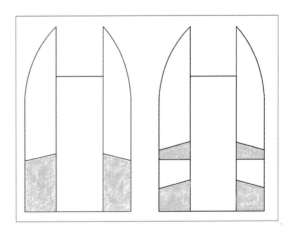

The on-the-water footprints for a stepped and non-stepped cat hull.

racing classes for them in the UK and Europe, unlike in the USA.

Catamarans are usually fairly faithful renditions of full-size offshore super cats. There are no official cat racing classes in Europe, but in the UK there is a cat class for the national championships. In the USA, cats are becoming very popular in straight-line speed records. Both cats and tunnels can be made to go very fast indeed in the right water conditions, and do not bank in a turn so do not suffer too much from the same rudder-induced handling problems as monos. The wide track and sharp edges on the sponson running surfaces mean that this type of boat can be very tight-turning – much tighter than a non-stepped deep V, for example.

The deadrise angle on the sponsons of a tunnel or cat can vary, from none at all up to 17–20 degrees if not using steps. In general, the more deadrise angle there is, the better the boat will be in rough water. However, the fastest cats usually have at least two steps per sponson and flat running surfaces with an outer anti trip.

Hydroplanes

A hydroplane takes the principle of reducing wetted area to its extreme by riding on three or four very small planing areas. Hydroplanes can be grouped into scale 'unlimited' and functional outrigger hull types (often known as just 'riggers), and then further divided into those that fully prop-ride and those that do not.

Prop-riding hydroplanes use a propeller that is designed so that it generates an amount of vertical lift to support the transom clear of the water when planing. What this means is that the propeller acts as the rearmost suspension point, providing thrust and supporting part of the boat's weight and therefore reducing wetted area to an absolute minimum. Also found on some outrigger hydros are devices intended to be the rearmost suspension points, thus leaving the prop to provide thrust. For more on these, *see* Chapter 4, on drive systems.

Another type of hydroplane, not seen very often these days, is the 'canard' configuration, which

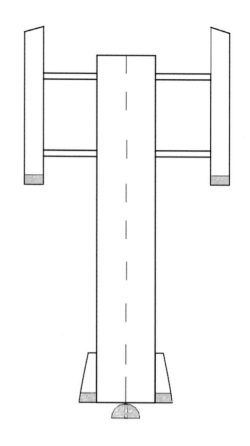

The footprint of an outrigger hydroplane is certainly minimal. Note the rear sponsons. Normally, the rear suspension point is the prop.

The underside of a stepped Mono 1 hull. Forward of the step the spray rails are fairly normal, but behind the step the rails are inverted.

rides on two widely spaced sponsons at the rear and one single ride area at the front. In effect they are three-point hydroplanes built back to front!

Underside of a semi-scale non-stepped hull, showing standard spray rail configuration.

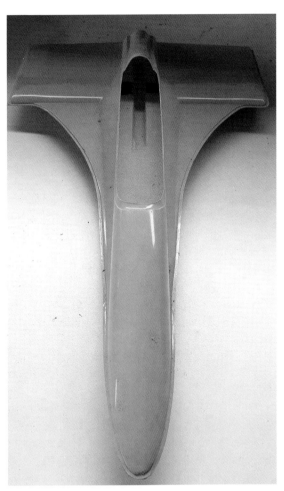

A back to front hydro, the canard hydro hull in GRP, for the Mini Hydro class. The narrow hull has a single running surface at the front.

Canards are not all that popular because, if they are not properly set up, they can exhibit peculiar handling characteristics. In addition, they generally seem to run slightly 'wetter' than a conventional 'rigger, so are not quite as quick.

Most scale hydro designs use more conventional props, which provide little or no lift and therefore ride permanently or intermittently on the rear of the hull. Scale boats are often slower and handle less well than outriggers due to their narrower track. However, they are considerably more pleasing to look at. Scale boats, in common with the full-size American 'unlimited' circuit

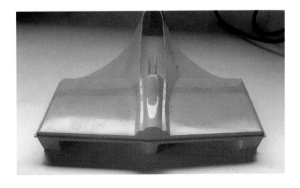

The same canard hull from the rear, showing the small sponson at the back.

The Firefox canard from Hydro & Marine in Germany.

The OBL Outlaw, an RTR kit moulded in plastic. It is a really good boat, but it would not last long in a racing scenario; moulded in FRP, it could have made a decent race boat. It comes with a small outrunner brushless motor but could probably handle something bigger.

racing hydroplanes, trap air between their sponsons to generate aerodynamic lift. The sponsons on most scale designs have moderate deadrise angles, up to a maximum of about 5 degrees, but typically an outrigger has no deadrise angle at all on its sponsons. However, it may well have an anti-trip angle. This allows the outside sponson to slide slightly in a turn and helps to prevent the sponson chine digging in and possibly flipping the boat.

The hydroplane may be the fastest of the three hull types, but it is also the least manoeuvrable and needs a bit of room to turn at full speed. Hydroplanes really are 'all or nothing' boats, and only work properly at full speed. Below a certain speed, a hydro will drop completely off the plane, becoming a hugely inefficient displacement hull.

My venerable Mini Mono, showing that some boats can fly! It is an ETTI Mini Envoy and has been a good boat over a number of seasons.

AERODYNAMIC EFFECTS

The aerodynamic forces acting on a boat tend to be insignificant at low speed, but can become a serious problem as that speed increases. At high speeds, any boat that traps air to generate aerodynamic lift becomes very vulnerable to gusts of wind or rough water. At high speed, simply keeping the boat on the water can become difficult, even in flat calm conditions. Cats and tunnels are particularly prone to this, as are scale-type hydros to a certain extent.

With monos, the more freeboard a boat has, the more it will be prone to 'weathercocking' in

A rather unusual stepped mono, the Rasch Essenz. It is virtually winged and has a narrow planing section. It is quite a competitive boat.

windy conditions. The operator will find they have to use the rudder more to keep the boat tracking straight. This is one reason why racing monos have very little freeboard.

The underside of a twin-stepped semi-scale cat.

An old TFL Apparition cat – a very competitive boat in the UK.

A very nice scale F1 tunnel hull that runs very well. Unfortunately, there is no MPBA racing class for outboards.

Another problem with tunnels and hydros, which is only really experienced at high speed, is the lift generated by the edges of the sponsons in a turn. When turning, the airflow is no longer over the longitudinal centreline of the boat. At high speed, the airflow around and over the edges of the sponsons can lift the outside of the boat, allowing air to flow under the boat, which may

Two Electro-Marine outrigger hydros of my own design from the early 1990s. They look old-fashioned now!

cause it to flip over. The problem can be avoided by rounding off or chamfering the outside edges of the sponson tops, to allow air to 'bleed' over the sponson top, thus reducing lift. This is mainly applicable to traditional wooden-built outrigger hydros. Most moulded 'riggers these days have a very futuristic design; sometimes the aim is to achieve a certain look, but most often it is to control the aero effect and keep the boat planted in turns, especially at the high speeds at which these boats operate. However, it is worth remembering that a well-designed wooden boat can be equally fast!

ACHIEVING HIGH SPEEDS AND EFFICIENCY

As everybody in the competition world is using high-performance brushless motors, the only limiting factors on power output and top speed are the physical limitations of the cell packs and the effectiveness of the hull design. The current world record at the time of writing is held by Joerg Mrkwitschka from Germany, with a speed of just a few tenths under 206mph, achieved at the 2018 Munich SAW. The boat was a self-designed and manufactured outrigger hydro with a single brushless motor on eight LiPo cells. This level of performance requires a significant amount of knowledge and persistence, not to mention money! Whilst SAWS-type running is becoming popular, especially in the USA, most people are happy with a decent speed and run time.

Quite simply, there is a trade-off between run time and power. It is possible to have a lot of power for a short time or less power for a long time, but, while the technology is much better than a few years ago, until it moves even further forward it is not yet possible to have a lot of power for a long time. The trick with a competition boat, which has to run for a fixed time limit, is to extract as much power and speed as possible, while maintaining enough run time to complete the race. This may mean juggling with prop sizes or a different motor, or both.

The Arcas: very futuristic-looking and very fast, if a little fragile.

The Arcas doing what it does best. It is a very fast and agile race boat.

Efficiency is a measure of how much energy is lost as waste heat when it is converted from one form to another. This happens in the cell pack, which converts chemical energy into electrical energy, and in the motor, which converts electrical energy into rotational movement. The drive system then transfers energy to the propeller, where some more will be lost due to friction and propeller slippage.

Even with the brushless motor power that is now available, the energy must be utilised as efficiently as possible and not squandered as heat due to friction and drag. Achieving the highest speed requires the use of the most efficient cells, motor, cable, connectors, drive system and propeller, in a hull that makes the most of the available power.

Really efficient components do cost more, because they are made from better-quality materials and to higher standards of engineering and design. This is why plastic kit boats in general have a tame performance when compared with a purpose-designed competition boat using the best components available.

CHOOSING A BOAT TYPE

Years ago, anyone who wanted a fast electric boat had to design it themselves or build one from plans. In the early days, there were no kits available and the 'Ready to Run' (RTR) concept had yet to be developed. Later, most plans and any kits that did become available were designed for IC engine use. Today, however, there are many different fast electric boats available, and the choice of which one to have will be determined by several factors:

- Is the boat to be used for fun running or for competition?
- How much building are you prepared to do?
- What appeals in terms of the appearance of the boat?
- How much money are you prepared to spend?

For a fun running boat, there are plenty of options. Most plastic-hulled kits and ARTRs are quite comprehensive and usually include a drive system, motor, speed controller, propeller and a kit of fittings and decals. Some RTR boats even contain cells and the radio equipment. Kits such as these also have good assembly instructions and do not require any real building skills, so are ideal as a first boat. There are also quite a few more expensive RTR boats available, many on eBay, that have the appearance of a racing boat. The main problem is that many of these boats have vacuum-formed plastic hulls and, no matter how good they look or how fast they go, they are just not suited to racing. A hull like this would probably not last more than two heats. Certain plastic-hulled boats might be competitive in terms of speed but would not be strong enough. There are always exceptions, of course, so it is vital to do plenty of research.

Choosing a boat for the purposes of racing can become a bit more complicated, depending on how seriously you want to compete. Competition boats are broadly divided into purpose-designed racing boats and a few hobby-type boats, with varying degrees of modification in certain classes. It is likely that a successful competition design will, if built correctly with quality components, perform as advertised. However, boats such as these tend to be very 'bare bones' in comparison with a hobby-type plastic-hulled kit boat, often consisting of not much more than a bare hull and a sheet of set-up instructions.

If you have decided you want to build and run an outrigger hydro, there are a few options, including pre-made commercial hulls or wooden kits, such as those from Zipkits in the USA (an online search will lead to other manufacturers, of course). Another alternative is building from a plan – there are quite a few available online, so a search should soon turn up something suitable.

Another important consideration – which many people never think about when choosing a boat – is the size of the water available and the typical water conditions in which the boat will be running. There is little point in building a hydroplane that is too fast and cannot turn in the confines of a small lake, or in building a small

One of Joerg Mrkwitschka's record-breaking outriggers. The design was more or less the same for all his boats, but one of them achieved 205mph (actual, not scale, speed!)

The underside of Paul Upton Taylor's Mini Hydro. Note the 'ski' at the rear of the boat, which extends past the back of the hull towards the prop. This functions as the third suspension point for the hull, removing that duty from the prop and allowing it simply to provide thrust.

A very nice scale hydro, pictured at a busy event, hence the untidy background.

boat to be run in a large lake where the water can become rough.

One of the best ways to start a search for a new boat is to make contact with a local club – the Model Power Boat Association (MPBA) has a list of all those that are affiliated. This will give you a better idea of what boats are being raced and find out what sort of components have been used and what modifications, if any, the owners have had to make. Most club members and racers will be happy to talk to you, although it might be best to wait until later if they are busy preparing for a race! If you are keen to get into racing, go to a club to see modern fast electrics running, even when they are not actually racing. This will give you a better idea of what is possible in terms of performance than videos on YouTube! Many clubs have one or more members who are into fast electrics and some even hold their own race meetings. Club racing is much more relaxed than national competition, and some clubs adopt a one-model class such as club 500 to encourage as many people as possible.

A whole bench full of Mini Eco boats ready for competition.

INCREASING SPEED

Making any boat go faster is often a simple matter of replacing existing components, such as hardware, with better-quality items specifically designed for racing. there are other methods for tweaking performance tweaks (*see* later chapters), but the first item to think about changing when looking for more speed is the propeller. Some cheaper boats come with RTR plastic props, which are usually very inefficient, tending to flex badly under load and lose their shape and pitch. While carbon reinforced types are better, the best option is a metal prop. Metal props do not flex, have slim bosses, and can be sharpened to a razor's edge and precisely balanced. Most metal props are made by companies that specialise in racing props and hardware systems, such as Octura, Prather and Dr. Props. A metal prop is usually the result of a significant amount of thought in terms of design, rather than being just another component in a kit.

The Helion Rivos, a completely ready-to-run boat that comes fitted with a brushed motor and ESC plus the NiMh pack. An upgrade pack is available, with an outrunner brushless motor and ESC as well as a LiPo battery. With its plastic moulded hull, it is not really a competition boat, but it represents a very good step up from a 'toy' boat.

For those who simply want something to play with at the weekend and are not interested in racing, there are plenty of good fun boats available on eBay, for example. The design brief of most of these boats will often have been to give maximum run time rather than pure speed, and this means that the motor included will not be very exciting. Often, it will be nothing more than a standard brushed motor with a fancy label. Replacing this with a brushless motor (even a cheap one) will boost performance considerably, often giving longer run time as well as greater speed. However, it is worth bearing in mind that a more powerful replacement brushed motor will more than likely be drawing more current and could be much harder on the original wiring and speed controller. Also, a brushless motor will need a brushless ESC, as it will not work with an ordinary brushed-type ESC.

At this stage driving a fast electric becomes 'interesting'!

Chapter Three

Hull Defects and Handling Problems

HULL DEFECTS

To get the best speed and handling from any boat, it is important to know how to check the hull for various potential problems that can occur due to bad workmanship or poor design. Hopefully, these may then be fixed in order to restore, or even improve, performance. When buying a boat, a thorough check of the hull is one of the first things to do. Many of the points made here will apply to both plastic-hulled boats and pure FRP-hulled racing boats. Obviously, if you are buying from a local model shop, you can save yourself a lot of time and effort by examining the hull before you buy it. If you are buying from an online seller or supplier, perform due diligence beforehand and only purchase from a reputable source, if possible. Make sure that you can get a refund if the hull does prove to be faulty.

A close-up of part of the B24's hull. The strakes and the ventilated steps are sharply moulded, contributing to the model's handling, which seemed similar to that of the full-size craft.

The Graupner B24 Batboat, a virtually exact scale version of the Ocke Mannerfelt design full-size racing boat. Although it was not made as a racing model, it held its own in races for a couple of seasons. The running surfaces of its hull exhibited some superb and detailed moulding. This model is unfortunately no longer available.

Poorly Defined Running Surface

A poorly defined running surface is one of the most common of hull faults. It occurs especially on vacuum-formed plastic types, but it can certainly appear on a poorly made FRP hull as well. Most of the cheaper fun fast electrics and 'toy' boats will be vacuum-formed from some form of plastic material such as ABS or similar and will often have been 'pulled' over a male plug. This means that all the sharp detail, such as rails, and so on, will be on the male plug itself and that detail will be transferred to the inside of the finished hull. The external detail will be left rounded as the softened plastic is stretched over the plug. If you do have the opportunity to examine the hull of a potential purchase, look out for rounded chines and spray rails, and especially the lower edge of the transom. If these important areas are overly rounded, do not consider buying the boat. If these areas are fairly well defined, with only slight rounding, the boat should be fine for sports or fun running but definitely not for competition. There are better ways of forming plastic hulls, such as 'blow moulding', in which a female mould is used, ensuring that the details will be sharper than when pulled

over a male plug. However, as this requires more investment in specialised equipment, this type of hull is usually only available from the larger kit manufacturers.

The strakes on the OBL Outlaw. Although it is not too bad for a vacuum-formed plastic hull, the edges of the rails are much more rounded than those on the B24.

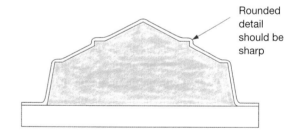

The outer details can suffer when vacuum-formed over a male plug.

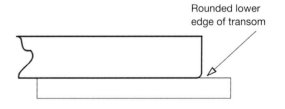

On a vacuum-formed plastic hull, the bottom edge of the transom is often rounded instead of sharp. This can cause handling problems.

Having said all this about plastic vac-formed hulls, these types of faults may also occur on FRP moulded hulls, for all sorts of reasons. However, in the case of an FRP moulded hull it is often possible to sharpen the rounded edges or build up the area with filler before re-shaping. One of the problems that can occur with FRP moulded hulls is when the hull has been removed from the mould too soon and the hull has warped as it was drying out.

Warping can also happen when building a boat with a perfectly good hull, particularly when the hull is made from thin ABS or FRP, whether that be glass or carbon. Because of the risk of introducing warps and twists that were not there originally, great care must be taken. To be blunt, it is quite easy to start off with a first-class hull and turn it into a banana! For more on this, *see* below.

Rocker

The term 'rocker' refers to a curvature of the hull, often nearer to the transom. It may be an intentional part of the design, especially in full-size boats, but in models it is most often a manufacturing defect. It has been defined on YouTube as 'a defect in the bottom of a hull whereby a part of the keel is lower than the bow or stern', but this would apply only to standard monohulls – in other words, non-stepped ones.

The area of the hull bottom around the transom on a monohull or tunnel is vital to the correct handling of the boat. If this area is curved or the bottom edge of the transom is radiused, the boat will 'porpoise'. This means that it will continually pitch up and down as it rides along. Boats that porpoise never reach top speed, are often unstable when turning, and are particularly vulnerable in the rough.

On a non-stepped monohull it is possible to check for rocker using a straight edge such as a steel rule. Small amounts can be cured with body filler. ABS

A slightly exaggerated drawing of rocker in a hull.

If the CofG is too far back, the boat is likely to 'porpoise', with the bow oscillating up and down and the boat bouncing as it is running. If the CofG is too far forwards, the boat will run very wet.

Based on a full-size boat, the ABC Hobbies Cesa had a vacuum-formed hull with a little rocker built in to keep the bow up slightly. This made the model seem faster than it really was.

hulls will always have a small radius on the transom as they are usually formed over a male vac-forming tool. A nice sharp edge can be achieved with filler or by adding a false transom from ABS sheet.

Most people have their own opinion on whether it is beneficial to have rocker in a hull, and on the effect that it might have on a specific hull design. The general consensus seems to be that it is neither bad nor good, but that a hull design with a small amount of rocker could work well in some cases with a specific operation in mind. Sometimes, a model monohull will have been designed deliberately with rocker, usually to give an impression of speed on a boat that was relatively slow. In some semi-scale kits of fast racing boats marketed a few years ago the hulls were quite large (often 30 or more inches), but the recommended, or sometimes supplied, power was quite low – often a standard 540 brushed motor on six or seven sub-C sized NiCad or NiMh

A rare sight: a double-stepped mono! This is a very good Nigel Bennett design.

A conventional single-step design looking a little 'flighty'.

Representation of a hollow (or hook) in a hull.

and therefore drag. The effect is similar to that of a large set of trim tabs.

The hull should be checked for hollows or hooks with a straight edge. Small numbers of depressions can be corrected with car body filler or by sanding material off the transom edge. If there are too many hooks on a new boat, it is better to ask for a replacement hull, as the amount of filler that will be needed to correct the problem will add too much weight. This type of defect can sometimes be hard to spot and is often the cause of mystery issues with performance.

Warps and Twists

A badly warped or twisted hull is doomed from the start – a boat with this kind of fault will inevitably suffer all sorts of handling problems. More often than not, a hull with a twist will only turn satisfactorily in one direction and may not turn in the opposite direction at all. Again, a good look over the hull before starting a new project may save a lot of grief later.

Boats made from glass fibre are particularly prone to warping, especially if the piece has been taken from the mould too soon. Glass fibre takes several days to cure fully, and the stresses and strains caused by shrinkage as the laminate goes off can pull the hull out of shape.

Outrigger hydroplanes can be very badly affected through being warped or twisted, especially if the ride surfaces are not parallel with the water. To identify any issues, place the boat, minus the turn fin and rudder, on a flat surface and check that each sponson sits flat. Rear sponsons should also be checked if they are fitted. Small errors can be corrected by sanding material off each sponson until they both sit flat. It is also important to make sure that the sponsons are parallel with the central tub.

cells (7.2volts or 8.4 volts). A moderate amount of rocker was designed into the rear section of the hull, to give the boat the effect of a bow-up trim. This made the boat *look* fast, even though it was not. Often, this type of hull did not respond well to increased power, having a tendency to porpoise and becoming problematic in terms of handling.

Hollows

'Hollows', or hooks, as they are more often known, are depressions or dimples in the hull, and can be the result of warping, shrinkage or the use of a poor-quality mould or tool. This type of fault seems to be more common with FRP hulls and is often caused by shrinkage of the hull after it has been removed from the mould. If they are bad enough, a hollow can suck the boat on to the water, causing excess longitudinal wetted area

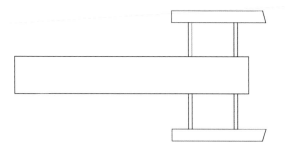

With a self-built wooden rigger, it is important to ensure that the tub is exactly square and the sponsons are perfectly parallel to the tub.

Warps and hooks and other nasties can easily be introduced during both the building and the fitting-out of a boat. This may happen, for example, during the installation of the motor mount, which carries quite a heavy load. This can spread by the use of a wooden mounting plate and this should prevent any warping of the hull. Styrene-based hulls can be distorted and even melted in areas by using so-called 'plastic glues'. Even FRP hulls can be distorted with over-enthusiastic use of adhesives that produce heat when curing. Built-up wooden boats such as outrigger hydros and cat hulls need special care during assembly to ensure a straight, true hull.

HANDLING PROBLEMS

In comparison with IC-powered models, fast electric boats tend to be relatively small in order to keep them as light as possible. A small boat is fine if it is only ever run in calm conditions, but it will struggle to stay upright when things get a bit rough. On the other hand, bigger boats tend to cope better with wind and choppy water. The best fast electrics combine light weight and a sensible size. There is no point having a boat that simply will not stay upright in anything other than glass conditions, so big and light is best.

According to Newton's third law of motion, for every action there is an equal and opposite reaction. This explains why a boat will experience various handling problems, due to the reaction forces of the propeller and other parts of the

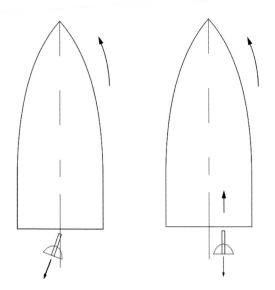

Two ways to stop a boat veering to the right when it is supposed to be running straight: either angle the prop to the left or offset the whole drive line to the right.

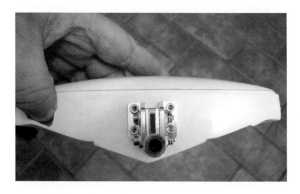

My Mono 1 boat during construction. The shaft is exiting the transom and is offset to the right, and the shaft exit is above the bottom of the V. The rails are inverted and there is a small lifting wedge on the right near the chine rail.

drive system. Such handling defects manifest themselves mainly on surface-drive single-prop boats as a tendency to want to turn right all the time. A surface-drive boat will also be a little reluctant to turn left, especially a hydroplane, which may trip over the turn fin if it is turned too hard in that direction. The easiest way of dealing with this is simply to dial in a load of left rudder

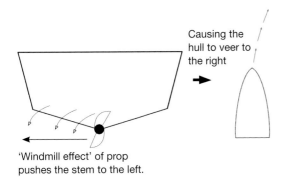

Causing the hull to veer to the right

'Windmill effect' of prop pushes the stem to the left.

Offsetting or angling the prop can cure the windmill effect of the spinning prop, which can cause the boat to want to steer to the right all the time.

trim. However, if the rudder is constantly turning left all the time just to get the boat tracking in a straight line, an awful lot of speed is being lost through drag. There are other, better methods of correction that should get the boat tracking straight with the rudder centred. Again, small, light boats will tend to be affected more than larger, heavier boats.

Torque Roll

Torque roll is the reaction force of the propeller, which is spinning at speed in an anti-clockwise direction (when viewed looking forward from the transom), forcing the right-hand side of the boat down into the water. This causes greater drag on the right-hand side, making the boat steer to the right. There are several methods for curing it:

- Running the boat with a twin motor drive with twin contra-rotating propellers: torque reaction is cancelled out and handling improved, with equal turns in both directions. However, there are disadvantages, namely the extra weight, drag and expense of two drive systems, the limited range of props available in dual rotation and the feasibility of running twin motors in some of the smaller racing classes. In addition, class rules may not allow twin motor use.

- Biasing the weight to the left-hand side of the boat: this is a partial or possibly complete cure, but causes a list to one side at rest. In the mono racing classes, all UK and European monos are self-righting and weight is biased to the left anyway.
- Small wedges (torque wedges) or ramps on the right-hand side of the hull bottom near the stern: these generate hydrodynamic lift and alleviate torque roll, but are a source of drag. Some experimentation is needed to get them right. This method is not often seen these days.
- Angling the prop to the left to counteract the propeller torque that is trying to make the boat turn right: this can be a good solution, especially on monohulls.
- Offsetting the drive to the right-hand side but parallel with longitudinal centreline: this is probably a better solution than angling drive for hydros and tunnels, but can sometimes be difficult to achieve on deep-V monohulls where the drive usually exits the hull at the apex of the V. However, this option is regularly used on stepped monos, especially those with straight shafts.
- Reducing the size of the propeller or using the same-diameter prop but with less pitch: the size of the prop in relation to the size of the boat can be important. Although props become more efficient as they increase in size, with a small boat it is often better to have a smaller-diameter prop turning at a higher rpm (revs per minute).

Prop Walking

Prop walking produces an effect that is very similar to that of torque roll, although it is less the torque of the prop than the 'paddlewheel' action of the prop pulling the transom to the left that steers the boat to the right. It is really only a problem with surface drive as in this case only half of the prop is in the water. As with torque roll, contra-rotating props, angled and offset drives can be a good cure for the effects of prop walking. In addition, the use of a three-bladed prop or running the prop deeper in the water can sometimes be quite effective.

Centre of Gravity

It is absolutely vital that the centre of gravity or balance point of the boat is located in the correct place. If it is too far to the rear, the boat will porpoise badly and be unstable; if it is too far forward, the boat will be hard to get on plane and will plough through the water, suffering a loss of speed. (Note that when people mention centre of gravity [CofG], what they are really describing is longitudinal centre of gravity [LCofG] – in other words, the longitudinal balance point of the hull.) The CofG can be altered on tunnels and monos to fine-tune the boat for the water state in which it is being run, usually by moving the cell pack(s) back and forth. In flat calm water, the CofG should be moved backwards; in rough water and when racing, it should be moved forwards slightly for stability and predictable handling.

Hydroplanes often do not benefit greatly from altering the CofG according to the state of the water. The balance point is relatively fixed on a hydro and is usually pretty much the same, whatever the conditions. Scale hydros can be difficult to get on to the plane with a very forward CofG, as they often tend to submarine. In any case, space is often limited with modern FRP moulded outriggers, which makes it very difficult to move things around very much. Moving the CofG on a prop-riding hydro may upset the depth of prop immersion and alter the handling. The transom may bounce up and down, or the prop may run too deep and load up the motor.

Care must be taken with tunnel hulls and scale hydros. Moving the CofG too far back on a tunnel or scale hydro increases the boat's angle of attack to the airflow, generating more aerodynamic tunnel lift and increasing the chances of a blow-over if it is caught by a gust of wind or a large wave.

Chine Walking

Overpowering the hull can result in an effect known as 'chine walking'. This is a rapid side-to-side rolling motion and is caused by prop torque rolling the boat over to the right. The torque is then forced back upwards again, causing the boat to roll to the left. The effect is repeated, often at an increasingly rapid rate, until the boat becomes

A representation of the action of 'chine walking'. The term refers to the boat rocking rapidly from side to side as it is running.

totally unstable. Often at this point it will flip over. Chine walking can sometimes be resolved by using a smaller propeller, or, if you are brave enough and know what you are doing, by using one or more torque wedges. Increasing the size of the chine and spray rails to generate more lift may also help.

Loll

The term 'loll' refers to the effect of the boat riding over to one side all the time, instead of riding upright. When the boat goes to turn, it will flop over and ride on the other side until it is turned again. Loll only occurs with poorly designed deep-V monohull models with excessive deadrise angles. If the CofG is too high, this may also contribute to loll, but this is rare.

Boats that loll are usually fundamentally flawed, and little can be done to resolve the issue, other than trying to install everything as low as possible in the hull. Adding or increasing the size of the chine and spray rails, to generate more lift, may force the boat to ride upright. To be honest, though, if a hull lolls it is more often than not a waste of time trying to rectify it.

Loll occurs when the boat leans right over on its side and stays that way until opposite rudder is applied, causing it to roll over on to the other side.

Chapter Four

Drive Systems

An electric motor converts electrical energy into rotational mechanical energy, which is then converted by the propeller into forward thrust. The process requires some method of connecting the motor and propeller together, preferably with the least loss of energy due to friction. There are basically two types of drive system to achieve this: the traditional submerged drive and the relatively newer surface drive, each of which have their good and bad points.

The installation and operation of the drive systems for the various designs of boat is a detailed subject. For example, the drive set-up for a cat may differ significantly from that of, say, an outrigger hydro. When building from a kit, following the instructions that come with the specific boat and hardware means that you should not go far wrong. Unlike some surface-drive systems, submerged-drive shafts and rudders usually cannot be adjusted once they have been installed,

so it is important to take care to get them right first time. If you do make a hash of it, the only course of action is to try and remove the shaft and/or rudder assembly very carefully, with as little damage to the boat as possible, and try again.

SUBMERGED-DRIVE SYSTEMS

Boats that compete in multi racing, currently Eco Expert and Mini Eco Expert, use a submerged drive. As boats in each of these classes are closely matched in terms of performance, especially now that energy limiters are being used, the only way to achieve success is to drive the shortest course on each lap, turning as tight as possible around each marker buoy. In order to achieve this, Eco boats must be well balanced, and capable of turning tightly, without losing too much speed in the turn. They also need to be able to accelerate rapidly out of it.

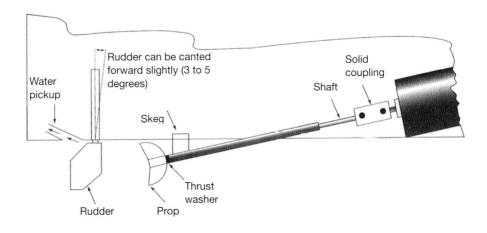

The drive train of a submerged-drive mono (Mini Eco).

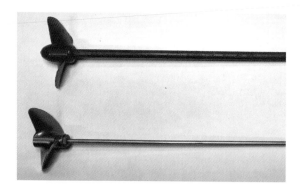

A size comparison between a standard 4mm propshaft and a 2mm wire drive.

A submerged-drive boat that has been well set up will give almost instant acceleration from rest and out of corners, with the ability to turn extremely tightly whilst losing very little speed. Unlike surface drive, submerged drive will work from almost a dead stop right up through the speed range.

The main disadvantage of submerged drive is the drag caused by all the hardware protruding from the bottom of the hull. This is often called 'appendage drag'. The top blade of the propeller is partially obstructed during each rotation by the turbulence and cavitation of the shaft and the skeg (the lower propshaft support). This means that for part of every rotation only one prop blade is actually producing usable thrust, while the other is still adding an amount of drag.

The type of propshaft that is most commonly available for purchase from model shops – a standard propshaft – consists of a brass outer or 'stuffing tube', a carbon steel shaft running in plain bearings (often Oilite) at each end of the tube, and a plastic universal joint coupling to the motor. The tail of the shaft will be threaded to accept 4BA or M4 size props. Standard propshafts like these are mainly used for displacement craft, although they can also be used in faster boats such as MTBs (motor torpedo boats), police boats and other similar craft, with good results. However, when compared with a specialist racing propshaft, the standard item looks very agricultural, being much heavier, much more noisy and much less efficient. Its greater

cross-sectional area creates more appendage drag and the carbon steel tends to rust very quickly.

Racing submerged propshafts are generally very slim and lightweight, to cut down on appendage drag, and the tube is often aluminium or even carbon fibre. Shafts are usually stainless-steel wire, often around 2mm diameter for high strength and to eliminate the possibility of corrosion. The thin-diameter wire will be fitted into a stainless-steel stub shaft (usually 4mm), which runs in a 4mm flanged bearing in the outboard end of the stuffing tube. What would normally be the inboard bearing is often only a nylon or similar plug – it is there simply to centre the wire shaft and prevent any oscillation. As solid couplings are used, often the shaft is supported at the top by the bearings in the motor.

Solid couplings, which are mostly machined from hardened aluminium, are so much more efficient than universal joints, which are noisy and, to be frank, unlikely to be able to handle the power for very long. In addition, the use of a solid coupling ensure that the motor is properly aligned with the shaft.

PARALLEL-DRIVE SYSTEMS

In theory, a propeller provides the most thrust when it is running parallel with the water surface. However, because straight shafts have to run at an angle through the bottom of the hull, some forward thrust is lost as vertical lift. This small amount of lift can actually benefit some designs of boat, but it does not help in all cases; in fact, it is exactly the opposite with some. To be honest, though, it is difficult to prove that it is this particular aspect of submerged drive causing the problem of an underperforming boat, all else being equal – it could be related to so many other issues. If it is identified as the problem, one possible solution is to use a parallel drive. This utilises a small-diameter flexible stainless-steel wire shaft or small-diameter (around 0.098in or 2.3mm) flexible cable drive shaft, allowing the propeller axis to be mounted parallel with the bottom of the hull.

Parallel drive was quite popular in the earlier multi classes, mainly due to the advantage it gives in the rough, reducing the boat's bouncing around by lessening the lift. However, modern hull design seems to have negated that advantage to a certain extent. Parallel drive requires more time spent in maintenance, as the flexi is made from carbon steel and needs to be removed, dried and re-oiled each time the boat is used. It can also be more easily damaged if the boat runs over a solid object in the water, such as another boat!

SURFACE-DRIVE SYSTEMS

Surface drive is so called because the propeller shaft is installed in such a way as to allow the upper blade of the propeller to break the surface as it rotates. For an explanation of the reasons for this, *see* Chapter 7.

Surface drive had been around for quite a number of years in the USA before it became more commonly available in the UK and mainland Europe. It is now extremely popular due to the significant advantages in speed it gives over submerged drive, making oval racing increasingly well supported. A surface-drive system allows a boat to go faster than one of equal power with submerged drive. However, this is at the expense of less precise handling. No surface-drive boat likes turning really tightly, as it will lose speed due to prop slippage. In addition, surface drive does not work all that well at part-throttle and at low speed – the design is about efficiency at high speed.

MOUNTING THE DRIVE SYSTEM AND RUDDER

A typical drive system consists of a tightly wound steel flexible cable drive shaft running in a PTFE liner, driving a stainless-steel stub shaft running in lead/Teflon plain bearings or sometimes a flanged ball bearing held in a strut mounted to the transom with a bracket of some kind. Stub shafts are commonly $^3/_{16}$ of an inch or 4mm in diameter.

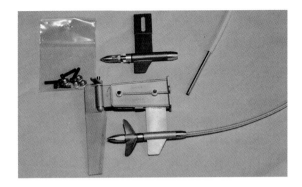

An Octura strudder unit (rudder directly behind prop). Note the flex shaft and the alternative drive strut.

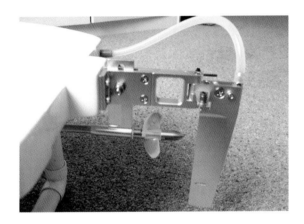

A much larger strudder on a 32in cat. The water cooling is direct from the rudder intake (ignore the green plastic prop!).

There are different diameters of cable available for different power levels, starting with 0.098in for small, direct-drive electric motors. The next two – 0.130in (3.2mm) and 0.150in (3.6mm) – are the most common sizes in use, with 0.130in and 0.150in just capable of handling higher power. Wire drives, which give a small amount of flex, are also being used, mainly for outrigger hydros. When they have been set up well, they exhibit the lowest amount of friction of any of the types of shaft. However, they can be fiddly to set up and seem to break quite easily.

The propeller may be threaded internally and screwed on to the stub shaft. More commonly, it is retained on the stub shaft with a nut (preferably a Nyloc type), which holds it engaged in a dog drive, which is usually a separate collet held in place with a grub screw on the shaft.

Earlier outdrive systems often used a strudder (a combined strut and rudder), with the rudder blade mounted directly behind the propeller on long brackets. As power plants became more powerful it was realised that this type tended to cause drag and slow the boat slightly. Alternatively, the rudder can be mounted to the right of and

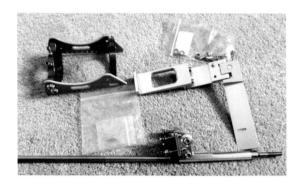

A set-up with an offset rudder for a mono hull. Note the water intake slot in the rudder. Also shown is a water-cooled motor mount and a stinger.

The rear of my Mini Mono, with an extended straight drive. The shaft itself is 2mm stainless-steel wire into a 4mm stub shaft. Note the helicopter-type adjustable ball link on the rudder arm.

slightly behind the prop, to take advantage of the less turbulent, higher-velocity water flow at the edge of the prop's thrust cone to give more effective rudder control. On a non-stepped V hull this arrangement will probably compromise the boat's ability to turn to the left, as the rudder will be lifted out of the water as the boat banks over, but this is not a problem to an oval racer, which only needs to turn right. Cats and hydroplanes usually have the rudder mounted to one side of the strut, flanking the prop.

Many systems mount the rudder with a bolt or sprung hinge mechanism, which allows the rudder to pivot upwards out of the way if it hits something in the water. Although all the hardware mounting bolts should be kept nice and tight, if the rudder pivot bolt is over-tightened, the rudder may be snapped off instead of pivoting.

LOCATING THE RUDDER

The rudder can be mounted on either side, but I usually mount mine to the right-hand side of the strut on all my boats – monos, cats and 'riggers – but not always flanking the prop or beside it. I made an accidental discovery on one of my monos. Having bought the rudder and the rudder bracket from different places, I had mistakenly ordered a bracket that was too short and the rudder was well ahead of the prop. I thought it would not work all that well, but I was keen to see the boat on the water, so I tried it. Despite my very low expectations, the handling proved to be immaculate both left and right and the short bracket remained. Unfortunately, the boat is now at the bottom of my local lake due to me trying to run it in water that was too rough, but at least I had learnt something. Having the rudder to the right of the prop has always worked for me, but I know that mounting on the left can often work equally well. Although there will be minor handling differences between the two options, it should not cause major problems.

Hughey Boats' single bracket drive hardware fitted to one of my 'riggers, and all the components of the drive. A very efficient, strong and light unit that is sadly no longer available.

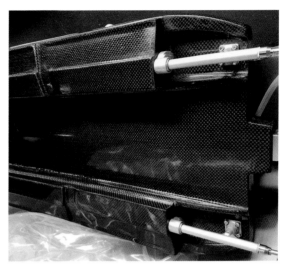

The underside of the Zonda.

My much-missed Mono 1, with stinger and offset rudder.

OUTDRIVE OPTIONS

The 'stinger' is based loosely on the type of outdrives used on full-size offshore racing boats. Sometimes used on RC racing monos instead of a solid straight shaft, it allows for a relatively small amount of angle adjustment, which is usually enough to fine-tune the boat. Stingers are more often found on twin-motored cats as per the full-size boats. When fitted on a single-motor monohull, the advice on rudder placement is still relevant (and I still would place mine on the right of the drive). When used on a

The type of stinger used on my Mono 1. The two brass objects are part of a very clever little dog-drive conversion set from ETTI. Between them, they convert a 4mm shaft for 4mm screw-on props into a dog drive for 3/16in props.

The back end of a Zonda cat showing the twin drives and central rudder.

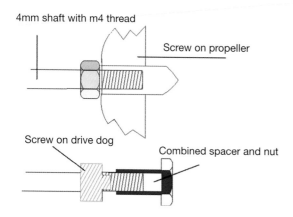

The ETTI dog-drive adapter needs a spacer tube to take up the slack between 4mm and 3/16in, but more often than not the threaded part of the stub shaft is not long enough. The other part of the set is a 3/16 OD tube with an internal 4mm thread.

Twin adjustable outdrive legs, which are very similar to stingers.

twin-motored cat, the rudder would be placed in the centre between the props.

One alternative to the separate strut and rudder is the steerable outdrive. Here, the strut and the rudder blade are combined together and steering is achieved through turning the whole assembly. Scale or semi-scale outboard motors can also be included in this category. Outboards are not used in racing in Europe, but there are classes for them in the USA, and outboard-powered boats can be quite fast. There are nice

units around (some of them quite expensive), and it may be worth checking out the internet for more information.

Other than outboards, it seems that steerable outdrives were mostly used on kit boats. Although there are fewer available these days, and certainly not for racing, they are still found on the internet. They are commonly made from injection-moulded plastic and are often semi-scale in appearance, resembling full-sized stern drives. The main problem with them is that they will have some kind of universal joint type coupling fitted, connecting the shaft from the motor to the outdrive, to allow the unit to pivot and still maintain drive. They are usually noisy and inefficient, and cause drag. There are several very high-quality and efficient steerable drives available, but they are expensive and made mainly for higher-powered boats that are often scale versions of full-size offshore boats. They have gearing in the drive leg but are not really suitable for electric oval racing.

Steerable drives can look attractive on kit boats and are acceptable up to a point, but it is impossible to ignore the various disadvantages. However, this is probably not the main reason why they are not used for racing, especially on deep-V monohulls. When a deep-V hull turns, it leans into the

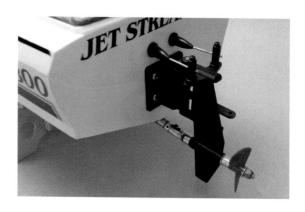

An old kit hull complete with plastic steerable drive. A drive like this should never be used for a fast boat.

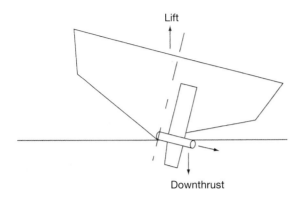

Lift

Downthrust

Steerable drives are no good on model racing boats, especially with non-stepped hulls. As the boat heels in the turn, the prop, which is now pointing down in the direction of turn, starts lifting the back of the boat. This causes instability and sometimes the boat will spin out as the front is forced down.

corner so the steerable outdrive will be pointing downwards into the water and this will lift the back of the boat, often causing it to spin out. This problem may not occur in a kit boat in as-built form, but it almost certainly will if a more powerful motor and more efficient prop have been added. That joint will certainly be affected. It is possible to use a flex shaft to allow movement of the steering, instead of that clunky coupling, but when more rudder is applied and the angle through which the outdrive is turned increases, drag in the flexi cable drive shaft is also increased. Good as they are, these cable drive shafts should not be asked to run through too tight a radius bend, as it can increase drag and also risks wearing through the Teflon liner tube. The shaft itself may even be damaged.

DRIVE ADJUSTMENTS

Most outdrive systems, including stingers, allow a certain amount of adjustment for thrust angle and this can be very important when setting up a new boat. A system using a strut and bracket format gives the most adjustability, allowing adjustments in both drive angle and prop height. The ride attitude of monos and catamarans using stingers can

be trimmed by altering the thrust angle. Angling the stinger/strut on a monohull or catamaran, so that the prop is pointing up a little, will result in the ride attitude becoming 'loose' – in other words, the hull will pitch up at the bow. This is also known as positive drive angle. It will decrease the amount of hull drag, but it will also have a negative effect on stability.

Adjusting the ride angle so that the prop faces down creates what is known as negative drive angle. This drive angle will push the bow of the hull into the water, increasing drag, but also emphasising the effect of the rudder. Too much negative angle will make the hull run wet and too much bow-down attitude may cause a spin-out when cornering.

With an adjustable drive strut, raising or lowering the prop alters its immersion depth, which changes the 'bite' it has on the water. This in turn has an effect on the acceleration of the boat and the load on the motor. An increase in the height of the outdrive will move the prop away from the water and the prop will run shallower. This may increase output drive rpm because of a reduction in load. A decrease in height of the outdrive will run the prop deeper in the water. A deeper prop will increase the load on the motor and will not always give extra thrust, depending on the prop diameter and pitch. As a matter of interest, if a prop of a much larger diameter than normal is fitted, the strut should be lifted to allow the prop to operate correctly. If this is not done, the prop will probably bog down, cancelling out the performance increase that may have been available from the more efficient prop. Of course, the opposite also applies: with a prop of a smaller diameter, the strut should be dropped. This is another good reason for using a flex drive system. If you keep the diameter of the prop the same but increase or decrease the pitch, it should not be necessary to adjust the height.

It should also be noted that some props have built-in lift to a greater or lesser degree, which can also affect the hull's running attitude. For most electric applications the propeller would initially be set to run with the prop boss riding on the surface, with only one blade immersed at a time. V hulls and stepped hulls used to have the shaft exiting the hull at the apex of the V, but this makes the boat prone to prop walking (*see* Chapter 2). As a result, most now have the shaft exiting slightly above and to the right of the apex, which helps to keep the boat tracking in a straight line.

UPGRADES

Fast electric drive systems fall into two broad categories: plastic hardware sets intended for mass-produced fun-running boats, and lower-volume metal hardware sets intended for racing and speed. Most mass-produced 'toy' or kit boats are primarily intended for fun running at speeds that are lower than those of a competition boat. Most come with some sort of plastic injection-moulded drive system, which usually works fine and will give reliable service at the power level for which it was designed.

When you want to extract more speed from a plastic kit boat, the drive system is the next component to consider replacing after the propeller and motor. Simply fitting a more powerful motor often destroys the standard drive system on a cheaper boat, but metal hardware sets designed for racing will easily cope with much higher power levels, will last a very long time, and will not waste as much motor power as heat due to friction.

The shape of the original rudder and the angle at which it is presented to the water may introduce handling problems as the power and speed increase. Unfortunately, scale appearance and dynamic performance often do not go together.

Unlike plastic, metal rudder blades and mounting brackets will not bend and flex under high steering loads. However, when trying to upgrade a 'fun' boat, it is wise to be aware that it is possible to spend considerably more on the extra than the boat is worth. Remember, plastic-hulled 'fun' boats are generally not very sturdy and can quickly

fail when considerably more power is applied – your investment in upgrades can all too easily end up at the bottom of the lake! Even if you have no intention of racing, it can often be more financially viable to buy a proper race boat. It will last much longer and provide more fun. One of my race boats is over ten years old and still going strong, having been raced hard all that time.

Full race-standard all-metal hardware systems offered by a number of specialist companies will easily handle extreme power outputs, and will do so with minimal frictional losses. For more information, head to the internet, or have a look at the short list of suppliers at the end of the book.

STRAIGHT (NON-FLEXIBLE) DRIVE SHAFTS

The straight drive shaft is solid and non-flexible along its entire length, from the motor coupling to the prop. Modern racing monos, especially those in the Mini Mono class, will use a 1.5 or 2mm stainless-steel wire as a shaft. This type of shaft is very strong and much lighter than the early conventional shafts, but it is not ideal for use with surface drive. A flexi-drive system with a stinger is preferable, or, even better, a separate drive strut on a bracket. Some people prefer a straight drive because it produces less friction than a flexi system, and is simpler and cheaper. However, all things being equal, the difference is not that great, and the advantages can be outweighed by the much greater adjustability a flexi-drive system brings. Still, it is always worth trying both systems and seeing which works best.

Another consideration is that, if you get the shaft angle wrong when building the boat and it does not perform well, there is nothing to be done except very carefully remove the shaft and start again. Despite the drawbacks, most European stepped mono racing boats, Mini Mono, Mono 1 and Mono 2 use straight shafts and of course if the installation is done right, they are very fast and handle well.

MOTOR COUPLINGS

The coupling between the motor and drive shaft is a weak point in many drive systems. It is quite often made from a short length of hardened aluminium bar stock, machine-drilled to accept the motor output shaft and the solid or flexible cable drive shaft, both of which are retained with grub screws. There are two main drawbacks with this type of coupling. First, they are prone to vibrating loose, especially where there is a lot of power and torque, as the grub screws can only be tightened so far without stripping the threads. If the grub screws loosen in this way, the result is usually the loss of a very expensive shaft and propeller.

Second, even if you do manage to wind the grub screws down nice and tight without stripping any threads, it often happens that one of the grub screws will damage a flexible cable. The end of each grub screw could be pointed or otherwise sharp

Standard 3/16in dog drive that slides on the stub shaft of a flex shaft. It is fixed using the grub screw.

A collet-type coupler similar to the Octura Flex Hex. This connects the motor to the shaft by clamping the flex cable, rather like a drill bit in an electric drill.

and will often part the outer strands and deform the cable. If this does happen, it is very difficult to extract the cable without destroying the Teflon liner! Not only is this damage to the end of the cable an annoyance, it also creates a stress point where the cable will possibly fail at some point in the future, when asked to handle any real power.

One alternative-type coupling that does not damage the cable and can be done up very securely is the 'flex-hex' or collet coupling. Several companies, including Octura, make a range of lightweight electric flex-hex couplings for the popular sizes of motors, to couple with 4mm and 0.098in, 0.130in and 0.150in cable. A flex-hex is basically a small three-jaw collet, similar to the chuck on a 12-volt electric drill, which clamps over the flexi cable when the tapered end is tightened up with a couple of spanners. Flex-hex couplings are still retained on the motor shaft with a grub screw, but are capable of holding a flexi with tremendous force. Although this type of coupling is not as cheap as the basic grub-screw type, it is worth every penny in terms of the replacement shafts and props it could save.

Note: fast electric racing boats do not use universal joint couplings. Even fun boats with decent power levels should not use them, but some still come with them fitted. They are to be avoided!

RUDDERS

The process that occurs when an owner initiates a turn with their boat may seem simple, but it is useful to have an understanding of what happens. As the rudder blade is turned into the water flow, the velocity of water down each face of the blade will be different, causing a drop in pressure on one face and a pressure increase on the other.

This pressure difference across the blade, coupled with the rudder's moment arm about the boat's centre of gravity, determines how the boat turns. The shape and size of the rudder are, to a large extent, dependent on the type of hull, the weight of the boat, and where the rudder is placed relative to the propwash. Submerged-drive rudders tend to be quite small as they are usually in a strong propwash and are often only turning a small boat that is relatively light. However, rudders for surface-drive boats are generally much bigger, even though they are mounted further from the centre of gravity and so have a greater moment arm or leverage. Surface-drive boats are usually larger and heavier, and when the rudder is mounted on a deep-V strudder (in other words, directly behind the prop), it will be working in very turbulent, aerated water. It may only have the very tip of the blade running in 'clean' water.

All my surface-drive boats have the rudder on the right-hand side of the transom, which tends to reduce leverage a little compared to left-mounted rudders. Too much leverage can cause spin-out in most types of hull, so it may be necessary to reduce rudder throw. With cats, the length of the rudder can add sensitivity to the steering, and that can cause the boat to oversteer or spin out, even with a small amount of rudder movement.

The angle at which the rudder is presented to the water will have a marked effect on the handling of the boat. If the rudder is angled backwards, it will generate vertical lift when turned into the water stream. Conversely, if the rudder is angled forwards, pointing towards the back of the boat, it will generate down thrust in a turn. The ideal position for the rudder is one that creates no effects at all during a turn, but this is virtually impossible to achieve. The rudder is always going to have some effect on the boat's running attitude when turning, and it will be up to the operator to try to minimise this effect if it proves to be detrimental to the boat's handling.

Hydros with a strudder (more likely on scale hydros), which creates lift in a turn, will tend to bounce up and down at the rear, often causing nervous, twitchy handling. Within reason, there can be a beneficial side-effect in cats, similar to

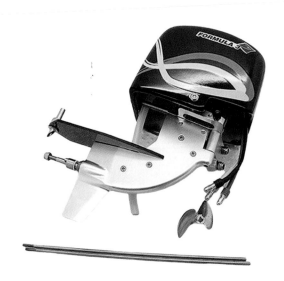

A TFL model electric outboard motor. The smaller of the two that they produce, it utilises a short flex shaft in the lower leg.

Two of the larger TFL outboards on an ex-IC mono hull. They have geared drives in the lower leg of the outboard and are quite powerful.

an outboard motor applying down trim before a turn to increase wetted area and thus tighten the turn. Generally, the greater the speed and the lighter the boat, the less rudder blade area you need to achieve good turns and the less angle you need to turn the rudder through for it to be effective. Strangely, a wide rudder blade turned through a small angle generates a lot less drag than a slim rudder turned through a larger angle.

Wedge Rudders

A wedge rudder is so called because, instead of being a parallel-faced thin flat plate, it is shaped like a thin wedge, with the trailing edge anything up to 4mm wide, or more on really big boats. Most surface-drive boats these days seem to use wedge rudders and there are various theories explaining why they may be preferable to flat-plate rudders.

A flat-plate rudder is supposed to cavitate towards the back of the blade. As the flow of water over it breaks down and becomes turbulent, it separates away from the surface of the blade, causing a lot of drag. Wedge rudders are supposed to stop this happening, because they keep the flow of water down each face under increasing pressure, stopping it from cavitating until it spills off the trailing edge.

With a flat-plate rudder, at moderate angles of attack, the water will flow around both faces without separating off. However, if the angle of attack becomes too acute, the water will no longer flow over the low-pressure trailing face but will become turbulent, eventually breaking away and cavitating. Again, wedge rudders supposedly stop this happening by maintaining the flow of water over each face, as the trailing face will not be at such an extreme angle of attack to the water.

The theories all sound perfectly logical, but they are not necessarily borne out in practice with models. In my experience, using both types on the same boat seems not to lead to any difference in the handling or speed. Interestingly, the late Ed Hughey – a man who knew a lot about fast electric boats – used flat-plate rudders on his own company's hardware. One of the pioneers of FE in the USA and the founder of Hughey Boats, he also used this type of rudder on his own very rapid collection of boats, all of which cornered and handled superbly at high speed.

Octura manufactures two sizes of electric wedge rudder, cast in beryllium copper, silicon brass or aluminium. Again, there seems to be no discernible difference in performance with either size. Virtually all the drive systems offered today by the numerous companies use wedge rudders; as always, there is plenty of information online.

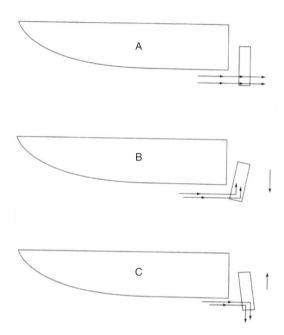

The effect of different rudder angles on a hull: in A, the rudder is vertical to the waterline. This may cause slight lift but should be the default position; in B, the rudder is angled forwards, allowing water to flow up the blade and cause down thrust. There is a potential loss of speed, but it can help some hulls corner more easily; in C, the blade is angled backwards. Water will flow down the blade, causing lift, which could make the boat spin out. Some hulls could be helped by keeping the bow down in a turn.

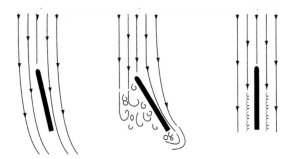

Demonstrating water flow and turbulence around a flat-plate rudder blade.

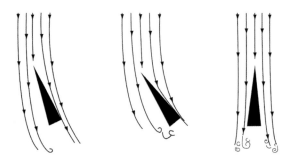

Water flow around a wedge rudder; the turbulence is reduced.

Rudder Linkages

Crispness of handling and responsiveness in a boat rely heavily on the quality of the rudder linkage and how well the rudder servo is mounted. Ed Hughey used to say that a boat should be very fast, but it should also be one that your grandma could drive! The only safe method of mounting a servo is to bolt it down on to hardwood rails or on to its side with a metal strap, braced with blocks of hardwood glued to the bottom of the boat. A servo mount can be made from aluminium or bought ready-made. It really does not matter, as long as the mount is securely fixed to the hull and the servo securely screwed to the mount. The linkage between the rudder and the servo should be a metal pushrod, ideally using the helicopter type of 'ball joint' on the output arm and the tiller arm. This will allow for a small range of adjustment for fine-tuning the rudder position, leaving the full range of trim on the transmitter itself.

High-powered surface-drive boats put quite high strains on the rudder in a turn. If the servo and linkage have any play or give in them, you will not get the full range of rudder movement and the handling of the boat will probably be 'interesting'. Also, thought needs to be given as to which hole in the servo arm is used.

TURN FINS AND TRIM TABS

Monohulls to a certain extent and certainly cats and tunnels have enough of the hull in contact with the water to provide this fulcrum. Hydroplanes, however, have so little contact area with the water that, without a turn fin fitted, the boat would just yaw sideways and keep going in the same direction when asked to turn, a bit like a hovercraft or airboat. Racing monohulls will also use a turn fin (or two) to help keep the boat planted in a turn.

Hydroplanes have a turn fin mounted on the front right-hand side sponson, as near to the centre of gravity as possible. They can be of widely varying size and shape. Like rudders, they are a source of drag, so they need to be as small as possible while still giving acceptable turns.

During high-speed turns the turn fin will be quite highly stressed, so it must be securely mounted. Scale hydros made from GRP or ABS

A pair of adjustable trim tabs. These are not needed on a stepped mono hull or a cat.

My Mono 1, showing the turn fin and the rudder's location far in front of the prop. It worked perfectly, though.

usually allow access inside to fit nuts and bolts through the rear of the sponson. Wooden-built outrigger hydros with foam/ply sponsons need a hard mounting point in the right-hand sponson for the fin; one good method is to use epoxy glue to fix two pieces of hardwood dowel through the sponson inside skin into holes pre-drilled through the foam with a piece of sharpened brass tube.

As with rudders, a turn fin will produce a certain amount of down thrust during a turn as water is deflected upwards over the blade. The aim is to find the best compromise position and fin angle that give the required amount of down thrust to stop the sponson hopping out of the water, with the least drag and speed loss during a turn. Too much angle will really slow the boat down so a bit of experimentation is needed. 'Rigger turn fins can also be mounted with the blade vertical – some boats seem to work best that way. Turn fins can be fitted to monohulls to stop them spinning in turns and to help them turn tighter. They are usually fitted to the transom on the right-hand side and, for V boats, angled so that the fin is upright when the boat is banked over.

If a second fin is fitted on the left of the boat, its angle will mirror that of the other fin. With oval-racing stepped hulls, however, the fin is only mounted on the right side and fitted so it is upright. This is because oval racers only have to turn right. In addition, stepped monos do not heel much in a turn, so the extra fin is not needed.

Trim tabs are used to control vertical pitching and are usually seen only on non-stepped deep- and medium V-monohulls. Fitting trim tabs to a boat effectively lengthens the hull and moves the CofG forwards.

Several companies make trim tabs from injection-moulded plastic with a metal turnbuckle for adjustment, and these need to be lock-wired in place to stop the adjustment creeping. Trim tabs on cheaper fun boats are more commonly a simple rectangle of metal, bent through 90 degrees and drilled to accept mounting bolts. This type is adjusted simply by bending it into the required position, taking great care not to inadvertently rip off the transom.

Trim tabs should be installed slightly less than flush with the bottom of the boat, ideally angled so they only touch the water when the boat pitches up. The tips of the trim tabs will drag in the water, slowing the boat slightly and forcing the nose down.

Trim tabs can bring a noticeable improvement to a boat that might otherwise be written off as a 'dog'. However, a boat that porpoises should first be remedied by fixing any hull defects or moving the CofG forwards, before any trim tabs are fitted. There is no substitute for a boat that handles correctly in the first place and stepped monos and cats do not need trim tabs! If a boat seems to need them, there is probably something fundamentally wrong with it, or at least with its set-up.

CofG FOR PLANING HULLS

Centre of gravity (CofG) is a big subject that could potentially take up a whole chapter and include quite a few calculations. For the purposes of this book, it will be simplified: briefly, the main

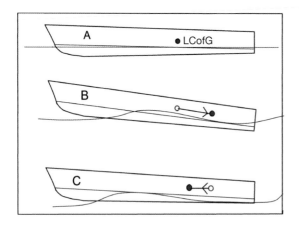

The way the LCofG moves as the boat accelerates on to the plane: in A, the boat is at rest; in B, it is accelerating 'over the hump' towards full planing mode and the CofG moving rearwards; in C, the boat is at full plane and the LCofG is moving forwards again (but less than it was at rest, as the hull still has a slightly bow-up attitude).

consideration with model planing hulls is longitudinal centre of gravity (LCofG). When people talk about getting the centre of gravity of a boat right, they actually mean the LCofG.

Monohulls and Cats

For every particular hull and speed, there is an optimum LCofG, but, as speed increases, the optimum LCofG moves aft. The diagram above shows a basic hard chine type monohull at rest floating to its waterline marks. As the boat accelerates, the bow will rise and the stern will squat. As the attitude of the hull changes, the LCofG will move further aft, until the hull gets over the hump of its own bow wave and the attitude of the hull becomes more stable. At this point, the LCofG will have moved forwards towards the bow, but not as far as its original position when the boat was stationary.

If the LCofG is wrong initially, it will cause problems when the boat is run. If the LCofG is too far forwards, it could run too wet. If the LCofG is too far rearwards, it could become unstable in turns, or bog down the prop. Porpoising can also occur here if the LCofG is too far to the rear. However, porpoising does not seem to be quite

such a problem on stepped monohulls as opposed to standard monos. (Any number of things can happen, of course, and it is not only the LCofG that affects the running attitude of the boat.)

There is a rule of thumb that applies to LCofG, which is that it should be around 30 per cent of the waterline length of the hull measured from the transom forward; this applies to both monos and cats. This is, of course, not a hard and fast rule, but it is at least a starting point! The CofG would normally lie in the centre line of the fore and aft plane of the hull. Its height above the bottom of the hull alters different parameters such as how 'tender' the hull is, roll rate, and so on. However, this does not really apply all that much to racing hulls, especially catamarans – the CofG in an FE racing monohull need not necessarily be on the centre line! As this type of boat usually has flood chambers on the left-hand side of the hull to facilitate self-righting after a flip, they almost always have a list to port when at rest in the water. This list is often considerable, as the batteries and sometimes extra weight will be placed on the left, to aid the self-righting action. This lateral displacement of the CofG would normally have no effect on the LCofG and will generally move back to the fore and aft centre line when the boat is planing.

The CofG may be altered slightly to allow for different water conditions: forwards for rougher water, to keep the hull planted, or rearwards in flat water conditions, to free up the hull. This is about the limit of what can be done with a solid fixed-angle propshaft, but there are other possible modifications that can affect and change the running angle of the hull. For more on these, *see* below.

Outrigger Hydros

The calculation for the CofG on a 'rigger is different from that for a mono or cat hull. It is normally stated as 15 to 20 per cent of the waterplane distance. Unlike the CofG on a monohull, in this case it is measured backwards from the rear of the front sponsons towards the rearmost suspension point of the hull (the waterplane distance). The rear suspension point could be a ski ramp or rear sponsons, or simply the prop itself.

Hydroplanes do not usually benefit all that much from alterations to the CofG. The balance point is usually fairly fixed on a hydro and more or less has to be designed in. It is virtually the same, whatever the running conditions, although there is a little wriggle room. It can be difficult to get a scale hydro on to the plane with a very forward CofG, as it will tend to submarine. With an outrigger, space is often limited, making it almost impossible to carry out adjustments. One of the worst issues with a 'rigger is to have the CofG too far forward, as this will cause the rear of the boat to bounce up and down.

MAINTENANCE

The ongoing maintenance of a drive system requires nothing more than re-oiling the drive shaft and checking that the mounting bolts and coupling are tight. Many flexible cable shafts are made from carbon steel, which will corrode badly if left wet, so it is worth making the effort to remove the shaft after each day's boating to dry it off and re-oil it. The best sort of oil to use is one containing PTFE. The Triflow brand is very good and is available from many model shops and, of course, online.

Lead Teflon plain bearings in the strut may become worn and loose after a while. Replacement is relatively easy: simply drift out the old ones and carefully tap in some new ones. Equally, flanged ball races used with a solid shaft will need replacing eventually.

The PTFE liner in which the flexi-cable runs will eventually wear through, so it should be pulled out occasionally for inspection.

It is very unusual to have a boat that does not draw up some water through the drive and usually there is not a lot that can be done about it. Pieces of wadded tissue paper may be used to soak up any water that does get into the hull, especially in the corners where the water will drain, but this is not fool-proof!

A helping hand lining up the motor and shaft during the 2022 MPBA Nationals. Of course, it was after the racing for the day!

Chapter Five

Brushed Motors and Electronic Speed Controllers

In the early years of this century, brushless motors were in their infancy and almost everyone ran brushed motors of one type or another in their boats. One big problem for racers was that these motors were almost always stressed to the limit and required a lot of maintenance – replacing the brushes when they wore down, skimming the commutator (usually on a special miniature lathe, for the same reason), altering the timing, and so on. It was all quite technical and could be quite intricate in some cases. As brushless motors became increasingly available, brushed motors were abandoned by racers, to the point that nobody races them today. In almost every case, if you are upgrading a boat's power plant, brushless would be the way to go.

However, some words on brushed motors still have a place here, as quite a few of the toy and fun boats, especially ARTR and RTR types, may well come fitted with this type. For this reason, it is useful to give at least a flavour of how they work, and this will also allow you to compare and contrast them with brushless motors (see Chapter 6). Brushed motor speed controllers will also be covered here.

BRUSHED MOTORS
Basic Theory and Construction

In an electric motor the electrical energy supplied from the cell pack is converted into rotational

Section through a brushed motor.

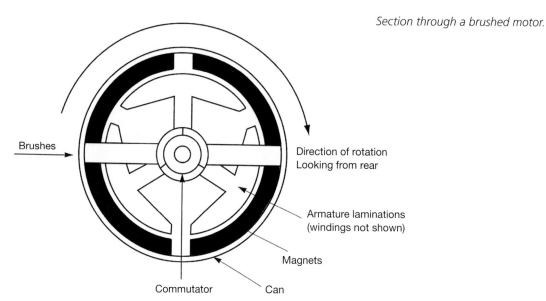

Brushes

Direction of rotation
Looking from rear

Armature laminations
(windings not shown)

Magnets

Commutator   Can

The armature and end plate with the rear bearing and fixed brushes. The end plate of a sealed-can motor is not normally removable but the securing tabs have been cut off in this case.

A sealed-can brushed motor of late 1970s vintage.

A view inside the brushed motor, looking from the rear. The dark curved shapes are the magnets. The front bearing, a plain Oilite item, is visible, as are the crimps to fix it in place.

The same motor with the armature fitted. Although the armature is not being held central without the rear bearing, there is very little clearance between the armature and the magnets.

movement by the action of magnetic fields created in the armature laminations opposing the field of the permanent magnets in the motor casing. The subject of electric motors can be a complex one, and more detailed information can be found in books and of course online. Undoubtedly, some of the motors used pre-brushless are no longer available, but you may find it interesting to read about the theory and history.

The typical brushed electric motor usually used for cheaper RC models is basically a metal can with curved magnets fixed to the inner wall of the can. Inside is an armature that is wound with coated copper wire and mounted on a shaft that rotates between two bearings, one in the front of the motor and one in the rear end bell. This is plastic and crimped in place on the can. The end bell also holds the brushes, which are carbon-based and spring-loaded to bear on the commutator. This is the rearward part of the armature, where the wires are terminated.

NUMBERS AND CODES: MOTORS

Motors were and still are referred to by numbers such as 380, 385, 540, 550, and so on, up to the Graupner 700 BB Turbo in various versions. These are all Mabuchi-type enclosed-can motors. In all probability, these days there will be no indication of the armature windings.

Mabuchi motors had a ten- to thirteen-character code. The first six characters related to the physical structure and the last three to six numbers related to the armature wire. The codes were really only of interest to firms specifying motors for purchase in large numbers from the manufacturer, but it is interesting to note what those three enigmatic digits mean. The first refers to the armature diameter, the second to the can length and the third to the number of poles of the armature – zero equals three poles and five equals five! It follows that a 385 motor is a five-pole version of the 380. However, a 550 is just a three-pole version of a 540 with a longer can and armature.

If you have the right budget, Mabuchi will happily make motors to your own specifications.

A 385 (five-pole) motor. The metal sleeve with the label on it is called a flux ring or torque ring. It increases the magnetic field inside the motor, enhancing the torque. If the sleeve is removed from the motor, the revs will increase but there will be less torque.

Two more modern 385-type motors, without a torque ring. Adding the ring from the older motor only reduced the revs very slightly; the modern motors seem to exhibit more revs anyway.

Five very old brushed motors of various sizes: (left to right) a 385, 380, a special 380+ race motor, the Hummingbird 15 and a big Graupner 700BB Turbo.

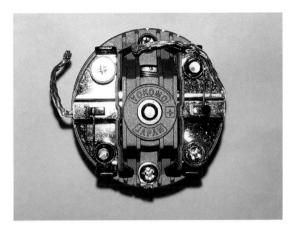

The modified 540's end bell. Note the replaceable brushes and springs and the rear ball-race bearing.

A size comparison between the Hummingbird, which was basically a 540 with a slightly longer can, and a high-power six-turn modified 540. The 540 is much better made.

Modifieds

Modified 540 motors initially were simply motors with a shortened can and a modified end bell. This allowed the brushes to be external to the can, thus enabling brush replacement. These eventually developed into powerful motors that had ball races front and rear and removable end bells to allow access to the armature, which could be completely removed. This led to all the various

modified armatures with different winds. The end bell could also be rotated slightly, allowing the user to advance or retard the motor timing.

Winds and Turns

Back when brushed motors were in their heyday and modified 540 motors were the thing to use for racing, the term 'wind' referred to the number of turns of the enamel-coated copper wire that was wound around each pole of the armature stack. The number of turns and the thickness of the wire determined the motor's free-running speed and its power and torque characteristics. The motor wind was referred to in simple terms. For example, '12 x 3' or 'twelve triple' would identify an armature with three strands of wire wound twelve times around each armature pole.

You will not often see this terminology being used today when buying a fun boat, unless you are going to fit a modified type of motor. (There are some still available.) Motors are more likely to be tagged as 280 size, 380, 385 and 540, and so on, as explained above. There is limited space around the armature laminations in which the copper wire can be wound and, with the racing classes for boats, not to mention the motors being used for RC cars and electric flight, there were many different wire thicknesses and winds available, depending on the performance requirements of each model. Given the limited amount of space, compromises had to be reached. For example, you could have many turns of thin wire or fewer turns of thick wire, or any combination in between that would fit into the space available. Generally, the higher the voltage demand, the more turns there should be and, naturally, the lower the voltage, the fewer turns are required. Motors are more efficient if the windings are neat and regular and if as much space as possible around the laminations is filled with copper wire instead of air.

Back in the 1990s, there were many different armature winds available for the 540 stock and modified motors, ranging from as few as eight turns up to as many as thirty. A standard sealed-can 540 motor, for example, had twenty-seven turns. Furthermore, with a modified motor, you could also ask for single, double, triple, quad and quint winds, so there was a huge number of combinations available.

In the old days, when brushed motors were the only option, boat owners needed lots of technical knowledge in order to contend with the various issues that could arise. Even if you are only using brushless motors, you may want to find out more detail about how things were in the past. As always, there is plenty of information in other books and online.

Free-Running and Stalled

One important bit of advice on using an electric motor is that you should not let it free-run for an extended time. Free-running basically means running it without a load. Avoid running any motor unloaded for more than a few seconds at a time, more especially when running at full recommended voltage. When a motor is free-running it is not doing any useful work, so all the energy it consumes will be turned into waste heat. Some motors will get very hot in less than a minute.

Modified 540s with low armature winds may have free-running speeds of as much as 45–50,000rpm and may be damaged when run free on a fully charged pack, possibly shedding a balance weight, or the commutator.

On the other hand, if a motor is prevented from turning – if, for example, there are leaves or other debris wrapped around the prop – its current drain will increase to extreme levels and it could burn out if full throttle is kept on. When this happens, the motor is said to be 'stalled' and in this state it will be drawing the highest current possible. How much current will actually flow through a motor when stalled is determined by the supply voltage of the cell pack and the armature resistance of the motor. A 540 on a 2S LiPo pack may have a stall current of 50–60 amps, which could fry the motor very quickly, not to mention the electronic speed controller.

SAFETY: MOTORS

Safety advice is relevant to everyone, whether they are a beginner or more experienced. It is all too easy to become complacent. The need for safe practices cannot be over-emphasised where electric motors are concerned. Fast electric racing boats are not toys and should be treated with respect. While IC-powered boats are very audibly and visibly 'on', so you know when to be careful around them, an electric motor can burst into life unexpectedly, simply by closing a contact. It will try its hardest to turn the propeller, even if that means going through a finger! Even a cheap toy boat with a plastic propeller could injure a young child quite badly.

The best approach is always to assume that an electric boat is 'armed' and ready to go. Never be foolish enough to try changing props with the cell pack connected. The slightest glitch could cause you to lose a fingertip. Simply switching the boat's radio system off is not enough. Unplug the battery so that it cannot start.

Competition boats in the UK and Europe have to have a removable safety link, which should be disconnected when working on the boat. Be aware that these are not used in the USA, or on toy and RTR fun boats, especially cheap ones from the internet, so it is vital always to exercise common sense.

ELECTRONIC SPEED CONTROLLERS (ESCs)

Proprietary Circuit Boards

If you buy one of the cheaper toy boats, the chances are that the ESC and receiver will be amalgamated on to a single circuit board. Even if there are separate units you will probably be given no information, other than how to operate them. Even the higher-quality (but plastic-hulled) RTR boats, which may have brushed motors, will probably have proprietary ESCs fitted. These may or may not be replaceable – and you will more or less have to guess at the specifications when trying to replace it.

The Feilun FT007 (*see* pages 56 and 57) is one of the better boats at the cheap end of the toy RC market. Removing the deck reveals a typical set-up for a smaller cheaper boat, including a very small brushed motor, probably a 260. From the steering servo going forwards, all wires go to the red box at the front, which contains some kind of circuit with a 2.4GHz receiver (RX) and an ESC. The box is sealed, so it is not possible to determine whether these are separate or on one board – if anything goes wrong, you will have to replace the whole unit. You should also be aware that, if you buy one of these types of boat, perhaps for a child, it will appear quite fast until they get used to it and want to go even faster. You might at that point think about fitting a more powerful motor. The trouble is that you do not know how much power the ESC and wiring will take, so you will have to remove the red box and buy a proper radio set and an appropriate ESC. It could all come to more than the original cost of the boat. It will probably be cheaper and a lot less trouble to buy a completely new boat and, if you are going to do that, you may as well buy a bigger brushless-powered boat.

How Brushed ESCs Work

If you want a more detailed explanation than this basic description of the functioning of a brushed electronic speed controller, the internet is a good resource. A brushed ESC is really just a high-speed switching device. It uses solid-state electronic

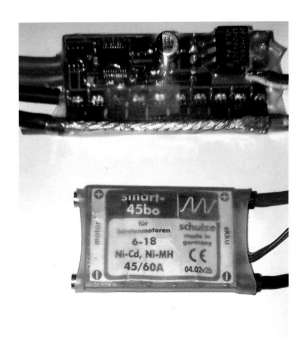

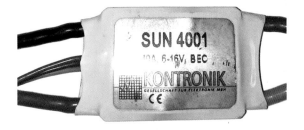

Three mid-1990s brushed ESCs. The top one has lost its label, but it is American, rated to 12 cell and around 75 amps. All the FETs connected by the cooling pipe are visible. The other two are German, with their ratings on the labels. The middle controller is rated at 6–18 volts at 45+ amps. It still works after undergoing a lot of heavy use, as does the Sun ESC, which is rated at 6–16 volts at 40 amps.

components called 'field effect transistors', or FETs, to switch the motor on and off many times a second, achieving motor speed control by varying the duration of the 'on' or pulse period of each cycle. The longer the pulse, the more current is supplied to the motor, and the faster it rotates. Ultimately, at full throttle, the controller is no longer switching but is fully on all the time.

Obviously, less on and more off (shorter pulses) means a reducing speed until at zero the motor is

These two ESCs may appear to be fast electric types, but they are not. They are on sale online with different names, but all rated at 350 amps. They work fine with scale craft, but you should be cautious about running them at much more than 20 amps.

An RC car controller. You can use them, but it is not advisable, as they usually have car-specific features such as re-gen braking and reverse, neither of which are needed on a fast boat.

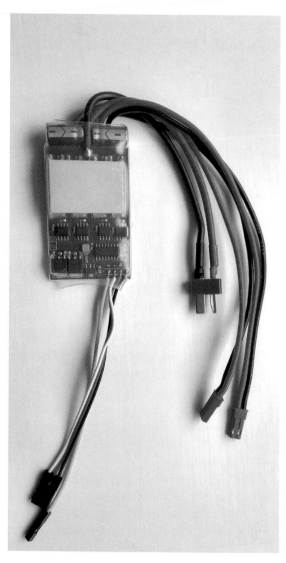

A small 20-amp ESC that features mixing of two channels. It may be suitable for a small MTB plastic kit, along with two very small brushless motors.

A small ESC may be ideal for the conversion of one of the excellent plastic kits of World War II fast attack craft. Rated at 20 amps, this one works fine and is now in a small lifeboat.

This type of 'toy' boat is a good starting point for a child, but sometimes there is a great temptation to modify it in an attempt to make it go faster. This may not be the best course of action...

The 'toy' boat opened up to show its workings. The motor is small and there is very little room for a bigger one. The red box at the front is sealed and holds all the electronics. Both RX and ESC might need changing if, like many of these boats, they are together on a single circuit board. The wiring does not look as though it could take much current.... In the long run, it will probably be cheaper and less work to buy a better boat.

stopped. This is known as a 'pulse width modulation' (PWM) controller. The rest of the electronics make it possible for the ESC to give a proportional (in other words, not stepped) and smooth control output, so the ESCs are often referred to as 'pulse proportional'.

This is an extremely simplistic explanation, but the subject will be covered in more detail under brushless ESCs, as this part of the control system at least is very similar in both types of ESC.

FETs

When buying any ESC you need to know how much current it can handle. FETs actually have a small amount of electrical resistance, of the order of a few milliohms. Greater current handling is achieved through adding more FETs, in parallel, to reduce the resistance. There are some unrealistic claims made for ESCs in adverts, along the lines of '360 amps continuous current handling' and so on, but if the claimed current was put through some of the controllers on the market, they would be blown sky high in an instant.

It is true that an individual FET can handle currents of as much as 60 amps, but only under certain controlled conditions and probably for micro-seconds. A more realistic figure would probably be 20 amps or so as an absolute maximum continuous current draw with effective cooling. If you parallel more FETs, their collective current-handling capacity will increase and their resistance will decrease. As a result, the greater current-handling capacity you need, the more FETs you must have in your speed controller. If a controller has ten FETs, for example, in theory that is 360 amps, as advertised. However, in the real world around 10 amps per FET is probably more realistic, to allow prolonged use safely without getting too hot. Indeed, it might be more sensible to rate that ten FET ESC as 80 or 90 amps at most, to give greater headroom.

Finally, really fast electric boats do not need a reverse, so do not get an ESC with reverse, or, if you do, make sure you can disable it. You are quite likely to lose your propeller and if you have a boat with a flexi shaft you could unwind and damage it by rotating it in the wrong direction. Do not forget that flex shafts are wound like a guitar string and are available in left- and right-hand winds.

Chapter Six

Brushless Motors and Their Controllers

Brushed motors are not used much in fast boats these days and the racing world, certainly, has almost entirely moved over to brushless motors. It is important to realise first that, while a brushed motor may be run directly from a battery with no controller, brushless motors and controllers are mutually inclusive. A brushless motor will not run without an ESC. In fact, a brushless motor is really quite a simple device, and all the clever stuff is done by the ESC. The term used by the model motor manufacturers is BLDC ('brushless direct current'). There are two distinct classifications of BLDC motors: sensored and sensorless.

BRUSHLESS MOTORS

Technical Explanation

The first difference that people notice when they change from a brushed to a brushless motor is the fact that there are three wires going to the motor. Those with limited technical knowledge may assume that it is a three-phase AC motor – it isn't, but then again it is, sort of!

A brushless DC motor is not a three-phase AC motor such as the industrial types used in lathes, big pillar drills and so on. In basic terms, it is only a DC motor with external commutation. The industrial motors are three-phase synchronous motors in which the speed is controlled by the frequency of the AC input signal. Brushed or brushless, the speed of the motor is controlled by the voltage

level of a DC input. That said, the only real difference between a brushed DC motor and a brushless DC motor is the location where the commutation takes place and how it is monitored.

Commutation simply switches the motor's current from one pair of the motor's windings to another pair. In a brushed motor, that function is performed internally and mechanically by a segmented commutator and a set of brushes. In a brushless motor, it is performed externally and electronically by the ESC and the motor itself has no physical commutator. The very fact that they both require commutation should tell you the nature of these motors, although you will see that there is an AC element at work in the controllers. (Note that by comparison a large three-phase synchronous motor does not require commutation.)

If the motor uses Hall sensors, which send back positional data to the ESC, then the combination behaves almost exactly the same as that of a brushed DC motor, the main difference being that the brushes and commutator have been replaced with their solid-state equivalent. It will be obvious to the observer that the controller will have the normal thick wires for the drive current to the motor and five or six thinner wires that are connected to the sensors in the motor.

Sensorless controllers operate on the same principle but monitor the rotor position differently. Obviously, when the motor is stationary, there is no rotational feedback or positional information. At start-up, the controller feeds low-frequency AC

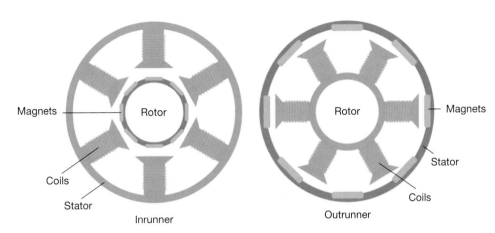

A section through typical inrunner and outrunner brushless motors. The disassembled outrunner is actually for an aircraft but has a bulkhead mount that could be useful in a boat installation.

into the motor to get it spinning. Clever electronics are needed in the ESC to achieve this. It is quite complicated and you probably do not need to be familiar with all the ins and outs in order simply to use the ESC; if you really do want to know more, there is plenty of information online. Once the motor picks up enough speed to receive reliable feedback signals, the controller switches mode and synchronizes itself to the motor's rotation. The controller must constantly calculate the time delay or phase angle required before each commutation. If the feedback signal is noisy, commutation may occur at the wrong time, so digital filtering is usually applied to keep the motor running smoothly.

A sensorless ESC has the advantage of not needing sensors in the motor and extra wires between the motor and controller, but its job is much harder. That is why almost all sensorless controllers use a powerful microcontroller with complex software, whereas, in theory at least, a sensored controller could be made from a few transistors and logic gates.

Construction

There are two main types of brushless motor: 'inrunner' and 'outrunner'. Physically, an inrunner motor is directly opposite to a brushed motor. Apart from the obvious fact that they have no brushes, the magnets are mounted on a 'rotor', which has the drive shaft itself central to it. The

A look inside a small inrunner brushless motor: the stator windings are fixed to the inside of the case and the magnets on the rotor revolve inside the windings.

winds are stationary, being mounted to the motor body on a 'stator'. The rotor revolves inside the stator windings instead of a wound armature rotating inside the magnets.

The outrunner motor is the exact opposite. Much like a brushed motor, the windings on the stator are in the centre and the magnets are mounted on the can. The major difference is that it is the can, complete with magnets, that rotates around the fixed central stator. Obviously, this can make them a little difficult to mount in a boat, and means that water-cooling of the case is not possible. outrunners and inrunners are normally mounted in the same way, using the front-face mounting holes. However, space must be left to allow for the can

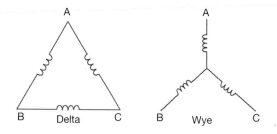

The two different types of winding configuration: Delta and Wye, or star.

A disassembled outrunner motor. The magnets are on the inside of the case and it is the stator that is fixed and the magnets and the whole case that rotate around it. The output shaft is mounted in the case and the stator has two bearings in which the shaft revolves.

An outrunner of a much squatter shape. It is specifically an aircraft type and it has a bulkhead-type mounting plate fitted. This could still be used in a boat but probably only in a slow-revving type.

rotation and the motor wires must not foul the can. ESCs for both types of motor are the same, apart from sensored types.

There are two types of wind configuration for motors: the Delta and the 'Y', usually known as 'Wye' or 'star'. Both will allow the ESC to feed balanced loads to all three phases of the motor. The major difference between them is the number of nodes. Delta windings have three nodes (A, B and C phases), while Wye windings have four (A, B, C and neutral). The connection schematic for a Wye winding is a star or 'Y' and the connection schematic for a Delta winding is triangular. Because many motors used in FE boats have low inductance, most of them use Wye windings as they seem to be more efficient at higher rotational speeds than the Delta wind.

Choosing a Motor

Brushless motors are now firmly established in the world of competition boats, if not entirely in the purely fun side of the hobby. If the last time you ran a competition boat you were using brushed motors, or you have never used a brushless motor, you may have to become familiar with some new terminology when choosing your unit. Brushed racing motors were mainly chosen according to the wind of the armature, although obviously the manufacturer's reputation was a major consideration, as was budget. The last two factors apply to choosing a brushless motor too, but the armature wind is not relevant, as they do not have them.

In some ways, choosing a motor now is a little easier than before, as brushless motors seem to come with more useful information than brushed motors did. Although the higher-quality motors will often have the full specifications available, more often than not the description will read something like this: 3565 4-Pole Motor 1900Kv.

A fairly chunky motor that would probably work well on six cells. The basic information that is required – size, kV and number of poles – is provided.

A selection of small brushless motors; the front two are outrunners.

A high-revving motor – three cells is probably the maximum you could use safely.

More motors from my spares box. The two larger ones in the centre have water-cooling jackets fitted and one of the slimmer motors has a cooling coil. Coils are slightly less effective than cooling jackets at reducing motor temperature, but they are certainly better the nothing at all.

What does it all mean? The first four digits relate to the physical size of the motor, with the measurements in millimetres: the first two are the motor diameter and the second two are the length of the motor casing, not counting the drive shaft. The next bit indicates that there are four poles to the stator that hold the windings.

The next four digits in this example indicate the rpm per volt of an unloaded motor: 1 volt = 1900rpm and 2 volts = 3800rpm, and so on. However, the motor manufacturers are not being entirely open here. The term Kv is actually a motor constant, but it is the constant for back EMF (back electromotive force), not applied voltage. The motor Kv constant (applied voltage) is actually the reciprocal of the back EMF constant. This may sound confusing, but the basic details are that back electromotive force (back EMF) is created when any electric motor rotates. It is this force that is used for electronic braking for RC cars, and it is also the force that is used for positional information in sensorless motors. If you can spin up a brushless motor that is not connected to battery or an ESC – with an electric drill, for example – and you can show that it is spinning at a fixed rpm, the motor will produce a voltage. In the 1900Kv motor, if you can guarantee the 1900rpm, the motor will produce 1 volt, as opposed to feeding it 1 volt to produce 1900rpm. This very simple explanation does not take into account iron and copper losses, or frictional losses, but the figures are accurate enough for normal needs.

Why is the Kv constant used if it is not the indication of rpm per volt? The thing is, the back EMF of a rotating motor is actually proportional to the speed, and the Kv constant shows the relationship between the two, so for real-world (rough) calculations, the Kv can be used as rpm per volt. It will always be just an approximation, but it provides a decent starting point when choosing a motor for a particular application.

Finally, excess heat is not good for a motor, so it is advisable to get a water-cooling jacket to keep it cool. It may be preferable to choose a motor that has its own maker's own cooling jacket as some aftermarket coolers can be a little slack on the motor can and will leak. You will have to seal the cooling jacket at either end with silicone sealer; it looks (and is) a little messy, but it does work. Using a cooling coil around the motor is better than nothing, but it will not cool the motor as well as a proper cooling jacket.

Explaining PWM

The circuitry that is the speed-control part of an ESC is virtually the same in both brushed and brushless versions – they both control the rpm of the motor by varying the motor input voltage. In both types of ESC, the rpm is proportional to that input voltage. In the past, mechanical controllers added resistance to the motor circuit to reduce voltage and thereby slow down the motor, but modern ESCs send on/off pulses for control. It is easy to assume that it is the frequency of these pulses that controls motor speed, but that is not the case.

At half-throttle the ESC applies full battery voltage in pulses for half of the time and zero volts for the other half of the time, but the motor will react to the average of those pulses. In other words, it reacts as if half of the battery voltage were being applied continuously and it spins at half of the full throttle rpm. The motor's speed varies with input voltage, not with the frequency of the pulses, whether it is a brushed or a brushless motor. The proof of this is that the ESC's PWM switching frequency remains the same regardless of the throttle setting.

PWM is 'pulse width modulation', not frequency modulation. PWM operates at a fixed frequency and only varies the ratio of the on/off time of the pulses within each cycle. To vary the frequency, the length of the cycle has to be changed, and PWM does not do that.

To recap, it is the average of the on/off voltage ratio within each cycle that the motor sees as its input voltage and causes its rpm to vary accordingly. The greater the ratio of the on time to the off time, the higher the average voltage and the faster the motor turns. The PWM setting in an ESC is altering the speed at which the pulses are sent to the motor, not the ratio between on and off.

ESCs FOR BRUSHLESS MOTORS

Setting up an ESC

On any new RTR brushless boat, the ESC will have been set up for the motor that is fitted and for the recommended number of cells. If you change the motor or ESC, you will have to change certain parameters of that ESC to suit the motor and number of cells being used. The Rivos RTR boat (*see below*), a good starter model, initially had a

The inside of the Rivos RTR boat, in its as-supplied form, with brushed motor and NiMh cells.

The Rivos RTR boat with the manufacturer's brushless upgrade fitted. The upgrade pack comes with the outrunner motor, a new water-cooled motor mount, a new coupling, extra wire, a 40-amp brushless ESC and a 3S 3600 LiPo battery. It livens up the boat and makes it a good choice for a young teenager as a step up from their first toy model.

A collection of my well-used ESCs (these are spares): 40-amp at the top to 220-amp at the bottom.

brushed motor and ESC but the upgraded version uses a brushless outrunner and ESC. The point is that the ESCs on both versions are pre-set, with no way to alter settings.

Some RTR boats, especially the cheaper fun-type boats, will have an ESC that is not in any way 'tweakable', so it cannot be fine-tuned. This can be frustrating, as several would certainly profit from some tuning. ESCs are not always well matched to the motor and can get quite hot, especially when an aftermarket prop has been fitted in an attempt to go faster. (By the way, it is advisable always to buy a proper water-cooled ESC designed for

boat use.) Other types, especially aircraft types, can be modified by adding a water-cooling plate to the heatsink of the ESC, but it is not really worth the bother. A proper marine ESC will always be better, especially in competition racing.

Every ESC should come with instructions on how to set it up with your transmitter. Some of the better ones will have a more accurate way of setting up, such as a connection to a PC or a program card. Setting up an ESC with the TX can be a bit of a trial but is still a valid way (sometimes the only way) of doing it.

The chart below is for a budget but decent 200-amp ESC.

A closer look at the Flycolor 90 ESC, which is reasonably priced and works well. It is also really well splash-proofed, if not completely waterproof.

The 150-amp ESC in my cat. The four large capacitors that this version has fitted outside of the main case are just about visible.

The setting-up process is as follows:

1. Cell count settings: some ESCs say they have 'auto cell count' but, as in the example here, that is often only for NiMH and NiCad cells. The better controllers will have true auto detection of the number of LiPo cells in the pack, but on some you will have to set up the voltage manually for LiPo cells. Some, like the example here, will also set the cut-off voltage (3 volts per cell here), while others will allow you to set the cut-off yourself. *Never* set it below 3 volts if using LiPo cells. Use a slightly higher cut-off voltage, if possible – a minimum of 3.2 volts, but around 3.4 for safety.
2. Throttle setting: it is often better to go with the auto setting, as this will usually have a short ramp-up time. In the long to medium term, it can be damaging for the motor to use hard start and quite often soft start gives too long a ramp-up time.
3. Brakes: a boat does not need brakes, so set to 'No Brake'.

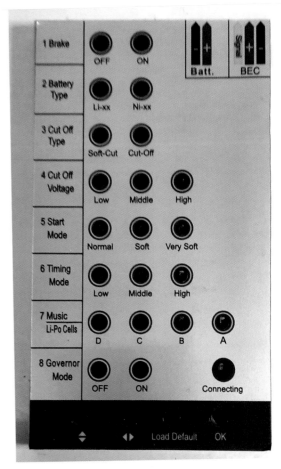

A fairly standard programmer for one of my smaller ESCs, which allows the ESC to be programmed to match the motor, in order to extract peak performance.

4. Rotation: this does not matter as you can change the rotation of a brushless motor by swapping over any two of the leads.

Although brushed ESCs can handle more than one motor, with two brushless motors you will need to use two ESCs. If you are using brushless ESCs with battery eliminator circuits (BECs), you will have to disconnect the red power wire from one of the leads to the receiver (RX). This is because you do not need both sets of power going into the RX and it can cause problems. It does not matter which ESC you choose to

An ESC can be set up from an RC transmitter, but it can be a frustrating exercise. The programming instruction sheets are not always easy to follow, but with a little perseverance, it can be done.

ESC Programming Chart

1.♪— For (2S-7S)-ESC **Cell Type and Number of Cells**	
• — 1 Short + 1 Long	NiMh/NiCD Auto Cell Count - 0.8V/Cell Cutoff Voltage
• — — 1 Short + 2 Long	7S Li-Po (25.9V) – 21V Cutoff Voltage
• — — — 1 Short + 3 Long	6S Li-Po (22.2V) –18V Cutoff Voltage
• — — — — 1 Short + 4 Long	5S Li-Po (18.5V) – 15V Cutoff Voltage
• — — — — —1 Short + 5 Long	4S Li-Po (14.8V) – 12V Cutoff Voltage
• — — — — — — 1 Short + 6 Long	3S Li-Po (11.1V) – 9V Cutoff Voltage
• — — — — — — — 1 Short + 7 Long	2S Li-Po (7.4V) – 8V Cutoff Voltage
2. Throttle Setting ♪— —	
•• — 2 Short + 1 Long	Auto Throttle Range
•• — — 2 Short + 2 Long	1.1ms to 1.8ms
•• — — — 2 Short + 3 Long	Hard start*
•• — — — — 2 Short + 4 Long	Soft start
3. Brake Setting (For normal Aircraft) **♪— — —**	
••• — 3 Short + 1 Long	No Brake
••• — — 3 Short + 2 Long	Soft Brake
••• — — — 3 Short + 3 Long	Medium Brake
••• — — — — 3 Short + 4 Long	Hard Brake
1. **Direction and Cutoff Type** **♪— — — —**	
•••• — 4 Short + 1 Long	Clockwise Rotation
•••• — — 4 Short + 2 Long	Counterclockwise Rotation
•••• — — — 4 Short + 3 Long	Soft Cutoff
•••• — — — — 4 Short + 4 Long	Hard Cutoff
5. Timing Mode Setting **♪— — — — —**	
••••• — 5 Short + 1 Long	1° - For 2-4 Pole Inrunner Motors
••••• — — 5 Short + 2 Long	7° - For 6-8 Pole Motors
••••• — — — 5 Short + 3 Long	15°- For 10-14 Pole Outrunner Motors
••••• — — — — 5 Short + 4 Long	30° - For 10-14 Pole High-RPM Outrunner Motors
6. Pulse Width Modulation (PWM) Setting **♪— — — — — —**	
•••••• — 6 Short + 1 Long 8KHz	– For low RPM and low pole count motors
•••••• — — 6 Short + 2 Long 16KHz	– For most out runner motors

disconnect, as the other ESC will provide power for the whole system.

Timing

Timing is the basic nuts and bolts of ESC setting. You can only time a brushless motor using the ESC and electronically altering a brushless motor's timing is equivalent to altering a brushed motor's timing by rotating the end bell. If you advance the timing, the motor will put out more power at less efficiency and run hotter. On the other hand, if you run the motor with retarded timing the motor will not produce the power it is supposed to. There is a happy balance to find when looking for the right timing. Sometimes, a motor manufacturer will specify the most efficient timing setting for its motor. Sometimes, as in the setting chart shown above, the ESC manufacturer will give a range of settings with basic advice on motor types.

PWM Settings

Remember that the frequencies shown in the chart (8kHz and 16kHz) are basically the speed at which the pulses are sent, not the ratio between on and off. Some ESC manufacturers give more options. A high-quality (expensive) motor may come with full specs, in which case the calculation Kv x Volts x Poles/20 may help. As an example, for a 550Kv ten-pole motor on high voltage – 12S (44 volts nominal) – gives 55 x 44 x 4 x 10/20 = 12210. The manufacturer might recommend a PWM setting of 8kHz with 5 degrees of motor timing. By the calculation, this motor should run well at a 12kHz setting.

Motor temperature and ESC temperature will always dictate the limits on motor timing and PWM. The higher the timing and PWM, the more power and speed the motor should make, at the cost of efficiency, run time and increased operating temperatures.

Of course, these are ultra-simple explanations. If you want to find out more detailed information, search online.

Disabling Reverse

If the ESC has reverse, it is advisable to disable it. Competition boats do not need reverse, and it can cause problems. If you are using a flex shaft, the winding of the outer wire is 'handed' and the shaft could be damaged by suddenly making it spin the 'wrong' way. You can lose the prop if it is screwed on to the shaft, as opposed to a dog-drive type. Even just going from full throttle to instant stop can cause the prop to unscrew itself. To understand this better, think about how you would screw a prop on. Looking from the rear of the boat, it would be clockwise (remember, 'righty tighty, lefty loosey') and when the boat is running the whole drive including the prop is rotating anti-clockwise. As the forces on the prop are pushing against the rotation of the blades (clockwise), the tendency is for the prop to tighten itself on the shaft. However, following a

sudden stop, the motor and shaft might do only a revolution or two before becoming immobile. The prop will carry on trying to move at considerable rpm and, as it will not be able to rotate the motor, it will keep rotating the only way it can, which is anti-clockwise. Of course, this is the direction in which you would unscrew a prop to remove it. That sudden stop/reverse manoeuvre is notorious for causing the loss of many props! Quite a few propshafts have a short thread, which only just allows a prop to be fitted. If the propshaft has a longer thread, using a locknut to lock the prop in place may save it.

Extra Capacitors

It is possible to add extra capacitors to an ESC, but what are they for and what do they do? Most ESCs that should be able to support high currents will have at least two large electrolytic capacitors mounted on the main circuit board. They are often visible externally and will usually have blue- or black-coloured casings. These large capacitors are there to protect the ESC's internal components, by smoothing out any voltage spikes. These spikes may occur because of the rapid switching operation of the ESC, which causes a magnetic field to be set up around the battery wires. This field collapses when each pulse ends, and this can cause voltage spikes into the ESC inputs.

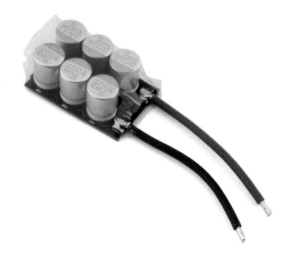

An ETTI capacitor board. Fitting extra capacitors can give the ESC more 'headroom'.

The question of whether to put the ESC near the motor or nearer to the battery because of space concerns, can be a tricky one. Deciding whether to extend the motor wires or the battery wires may have implications for the need for extra capacitors. 'Experts' on FE forums and YouTube videos will advise against extending the motor wires because that can cause interference. Others will tell you never to extend the battery leads because this increases resistance and can cause the spikes in the ESC to be bigger, which could damage it. Interestingly, it seems that much of the advice about lengthening the motor wires comes from aircraft modellers, where motor and ESC could be quite a distance apart.

There are consequences whichever way you decide to go, but it is probably preferable to leave the motor wires alone and extend the battery wires a little. In any case, in a boat you should not need to extend any leads more than a few inches and you should be OK up to about 3 inches or so before you need to think about extra capacitors.

If you lengthen the battery wires more than about 4 inches, the higher the voltage of the spikes can be and the more important it is to run the extra capacitors. The voltage at the peak of the spikes will be quite a bit higher than the nominal battery voltage. Using the capacitors will smooth out the spikes and help extend the life of the ESC. The one thing you do not want to do is shorten the wires from the motor for any reason! In fact, it is not advisable to shorten the three wires from the ESC either. Just accept that you have a little extra wire and find room for it.

Finally, the most common reason for using a separate capacitor bank in a high-powered competition boat is the momentary sag in voltage that can occur when the motor is given full throttle. Especially with a surface-drive boat, it is in a virtually stalled condition for a very short time until the prop bites, the boat moves and the load on the motor reduces. For a split second, this can cause the battery voltage to sag momentarily, especially on a battery that has a higher internal resistance. The usual result is a dropping out of

A capacitor bank can be made using electrolytic capacitors similar to these. Note that these caps are polarising; the white stripe denotes the negative lead.

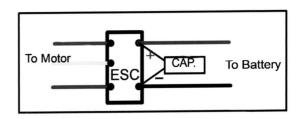

The method for fitting a single capacitor. A large capacitor bank would be wired in the same way.

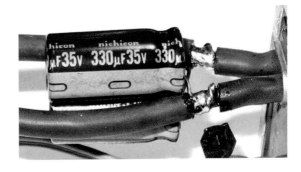

Two capacitors wired in parallel, giving 660µf. The caps have been spliced into the battery wires, which is a good method as there is usually no access inside the ESC and the caps should be as close to it as possible. It is normally simpler to use a single larger-value cap.

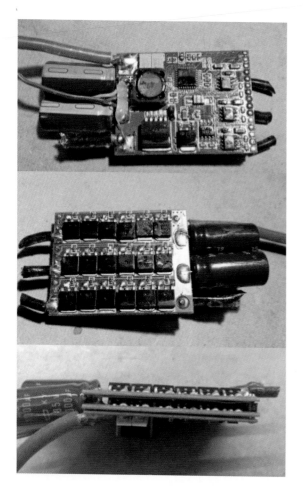

the BEC (battery eliminator circuit), which can stop servos and the ESC from working. This causes the boat to briefly move, then stop until the voltage comes back up, only for the process to repeat while full throttle is held on.

Having a capacitor bank will hold the voltage at the correct level for the very short time that is needed, allowing the ESC to operate correctly. The capacitors will charge to battery voltage and will be able to provide the necessary extra boost whenever the battery voltage sinks below the voltage across the capacitors.

A composite picture showing a 'dead' speed control and the complicated structure of brushless ESCs: (bottom) the triple circuit board construction; (top) the control circuitry; and (middle) the power board with multiple power FETs. Five or six of the FETs on the top right of the PCB are burnt out.

Chapter Seven

Propellers

The propeller converts the rotational movement of the motor into forward motion. The way in which it achieves this is another highly complex subject, but for the purposes of this book it is enough to know which prop will do what, not precisely *how* it does it. It may help to think of it as a screw screwing into wood, except that the prop is 'screwing' into water – indeed, propellers are often referred to as 'screws'. It should be said that, as is the case with the other components in a fast electric boat, it is vital for the best performance that you select the right type and size of prop.

PROPELLER TYPES

In the full-size world there are several subdivisions of props, but in the modelling world there are just two: submerged props and surface-piercing or ventilated props.

The blade section of a submerged-drive prop forces water to flow at a higher velocity over the leading or forward face, creating a pressure differential across the prop that provides forward thrust. Submerged-drive props tend to be quite small in diameter and usually have quite a mild pitch. There are several reasons for this. First, turning a fully immersed prop requires a lot of energy. Submerged-drive Eco-type boats always use direct-drive motors, have to run for over six minutes, and do not have a huge amount of power

to spare. A small prop with a lot of pitch mounted to a high-drag, low-speed monohull will be very prone to cavitation (*see* below) and a consequent loss of thrust and performance.

Soon after the introduction of the fully submerged propeller as it is known today, surface-piercing or partially submerged propellers (as they were termed then) were being proposed as a replacement for paddle wheels. The first patent for a surface-piercing prop was registered in 1869 and had several of the features that now appear in modern props, such as blade cupping for increased

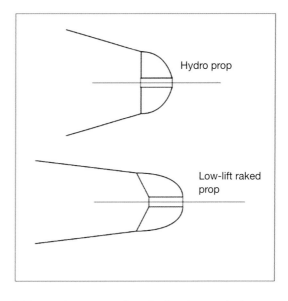

Different thrust cones for raked and non-raked props.

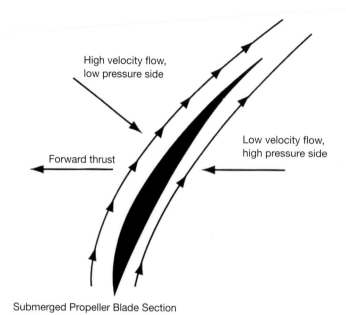

High velocity flow,
low pressure side

Low velocity flow,
high pressure side

Forward thrust

Submerged Propeller Blade Section

Sections through both submerged and surface-piercing propellers, showing the marked difference between them.

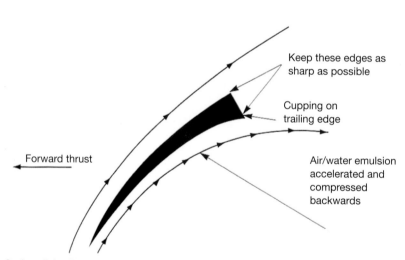

Keep these edges as
sharp as possible

Cupping on
trailing edge

Forward thrust

Air/water emulsion
accelerated and
compressed
backwards

Surface Drive Propeller Blade Section

performance. Originally, the surface-piercing props were being developed for use in shallow water, but as development continued it became clear that they had a higher efficiency than fully submerged props. As a result, the focus of the development shifted towards high-speed applications. Albert Hickman, the designer of the famous Sea Sled high-speed boat, used and further developed surface-piercing props to achieve high boat speeds from modest power. The first surface-piercing prop for RC models was introduced in 1957 by Tom Perzentka of Octura Models.

Surface-drive propellers produce thrust by accelerating and compressing an emulsion of air and water backwards off the rear face of the prop. Because surface-drive props work in this compressible medium and have one blade out of the water for part of each revolution, the blade drag is less than for the equivalent submerged prop. The latter always has the drag of at least

A Hickman Sea Sled doing about 45mph. It was designed and built by Albert Hickman and used, among other things, to develop surface-drive props. The hull was an unusual inverted V. Note the rooster tail!

A modern Sea Sled type being moulded. Looking from the front, it is clear that the inverted V flattens towards the transom.

two blades, plus the appendage drag from the propshaft, skeg and rudder. The result of this is that surface-drive props can be considerably larger in diameter and with greater pitch and blade area, without overloading the motor.

CAVITATION AND AERATION

Cavitation and aeration are distinctly different effects, but are easily confused with one another.

Aeration, or ventilation as it is sometimes called, is what happens when a submerged propeller is allowed to draw air down from the surface into the prop disc, causing a partial or complete loss of thrust. The plate fitted over the prop on an outboard motor is often mistakenly referred to as an anti-cavitation plate. It is, in fact, an anti-ventilation plate, put there to prevent the prop from aerating. The prop on an outboard is, of course, usually a submerged type.

Cavitation occurs when the pressure drop across the prop becomes too great. The boiling point of a fluid – the temperature at which it turns from a liquid into a gas – drops in proportion to pressure. With an extreme pressure drop, water will vaporise at ambient temperature, and this can happen when

A submerged-drive prop for Eco boats.

you have a small prop spinning at very high rpm or a prop with excessive pitch.

Cavitation voids are not bubbles of air, but small regions of partial vacuum in which water is momentarily allowed to vaporise, before the void collapses back on itself again under pressure. In extreme cases, these cavitation voids can envelop the prop disc, causing a complete loss of thrust. Cavitation produces an awful lot of noise and vibration, and for this reason the propellers on a submarine are very carefully designed to avoid cavitating. Submerged propellers become very inefficient and produce a lot less thrust if allowed to aerate or cavitate. On a full-size prop, cavitation can be very damaging and can seriously wear the blades away.

Surface-drive props are designed to give ultimate top speed and need to be aerated to work efficiently. Surface props do not work well at low speeds, which cause them to suffer a lot of slippage, or at low rpm, and, compared with a submerged prop, they give relatively poor acceleration from rest. Submerged props give near-instantaneous acceleration from rest and will work right through the speed range, from dead slow to full speed.

CHOOSING A PROPELLER

Propellers are available in several different materials. Most cheap RTR boats come with a plastic prop of some sort, and model shops tend not to keep the specialist props that are used for racing. Usually, they only stock a few sizes of plastic prop.

There is nothing basically wrong with plastic props. They do work but they are rather inefficient and break easily. Plastic props flex under load, losing their shape and pitch, and cannot be sharpened and balanced. Because of the low strength of the plastic used, the boss has to be extremely thick, and this causes drag. Octura make quite a few small-diameter plastic dog-drive props, with pitch/diameter ratios of 1.2 and 1.4. These are in addition to their cast BeCu props.

Graupner make a pretty good range of props in carbon fibre that are roughly a quarter to a third

of the price of metal. While these work quite well and are miles better than a plastic prop, they still fall short of a decent metal prop – carbon fibre will shatter if it hits anything. Graupner's carbon props are not ideal for racing, but they are fine for fun running, and they can also be useful when initially setting up a new boat. Again, the boss on a carbon prop will have a larger diameter than that on a metal prop.

A number of props come with a 3/16in dog drive, especially those made in the USA. There are smaller props, which use a 1/8in drive, as well as 4mm dog-drive and M4 threaded props, which are mainly used in the UK and Europe. Choice of prop size is determined by several variables: the available power and torque, the weight of the boat and the amount of wetted area, and hence drag.

The faster a boat goes, the greater the pitch of the prop needs to be. (Remember, this is boat speed, not prop rotational speed!) A surface-drive outrigger hydro needs a much coarser-pitch prop than a multi boat, as well as a prop that generates some vertical lift, to help support the transom clear of the water at planing speed. Cats particularly like props with a reasonable amount of rake, as they need thrust without too much lift.

Props that generate lift do so because of the shape of their thrust cone, and this is a function of their blade shape. The Prather props and the Octura 'X' series have a very narrow collimated thrust cone and so generate little or no lift. For this reason, and because of their relatively mild pitch, these props are

A selection of 3/16in Octura dog-drive props: (left to right) X440, X646, X648, 1747, 2047 and 1750. The last two props are unfinished – the moulding flash on the hubs has not been removed.

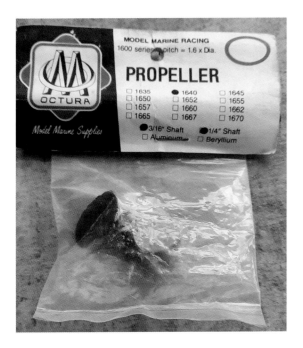

A 'new' prop, probably fifteen years old but still unopened.

primarily intended for monohulls and tunnels where lift-generating props would cause handling problems. These props are cupped to varying degrees on the trailing edge and give good acceleration.

The Octura 17, 19, 20 and 21 series high-pitch props have a much wider thrust cone and produce varying amounts of lift. These props tend to be very inefficient at low rpm and low forward speed.

The varying thrust cone shapes can be identified by looking at the 'rooster tail' of water that is thrown up by the surfacing prop blades. High-lift 17, 19 and 20 series props throw water much higher in the air than the X series, for example, which display much more modest rooster tails.

There are several manufacturers of props. Octura units seem to be widely used worldwide, while in Europe and the UK many people use items from Etti, Tenshock or Doctor Props. The ETTI and Tenshock props are mainly CNC aluminium and are very good but sometimes could benefit from a little sharpening. The Doctor Props products may be unique at the moment in that, while some are

CNC, some are 3D-printed in stainless steel and even titanium. They are quite expensive but do not need balancing or sharpening and can be taken straight from the pack, fitted and raced.

It is difficult to choose, but remember that you may have to try the prop at several different immersion depths before you get it to work, so do not throw it away in disgust after just one attempt!

NUMBERS AND CODES: PROPELLERS

The Octura, Prather and ABC ranges are identified with a system of code numbers.

ABC props information seems confusing but, when you know the secret, it is very informative. For example, '2716-10-50(2) CLL' indicates a prop that has a diameter of 2.7in, a 1.6 pitch ratio, 10 degrees of rake angle, a blade area ratio of 50, and two blades (2). 'CL' shows that it is a cleaver type ('CP' would indicate chopper) and that it has a left rotation (L), as opposed to right, which would be 'R'.

Octura props have a two-part code number that indicates the pitch – for example, X4, X6 or 1.7 (which also gives a guide to intended application) – and gives the diameter in millimetres.

Prather props have a three-number code – for example,

215	40.6mm (1.60in)	2.5"
220	43.7mm (1.72in)	2.6"
225	46.7mm (1.84in)	2.8"

PROPELLER PREPARATION

(Or, how to cut your fingers to ribbons the easy way.)

When you buy a new Octura, Prather or ABC prop, it will usually come in the 'as-cast' state. The boss will have been bored out and the dog-drive slot will have been machined, but the blades will need sharpening and polishing, and you will need to balance the prop before it is fitted to the boat.

A stainless-steel surface-drive prop.

An old photo from my collection (origin unknown): a submerged (full-size) propeller cavitating massively. It was probably a test set-up.

The damaged prop off my Mini Mono – it needed a little work to repair.

A magnetic prop balancer is an essential item. This particular model is quite tall as it is designed for aircraft props. It is no longer available, but just visible behind is the small balancer made for boat props that is in use today.

A prop that is out of balance will never reach top rpm; parts of it may shake loose and it may suffer premature failure of the shaft bearing. The best way to balance a prop is to use a magnetic balancer. The prop is mounted on to a shaft that is suspended between two powerful magnets. Only one end of the shaft is in contact, while the other floats in mid-air. Magnetic balancers have very little friction and can balance small, light props very accurately.

To avoid confusion, for the purposes of this book, the forward face of the propeller is the one facing towards the front of the boat, when the prop is mounted to its shaft. On a surface-drive prop, this face does not do much, as all the work is done by the aft or rear face.

When balancing a prop, material should be evenly filed or sanded off the forward face of each blade, checking the balance regularly as you go. Do not remove material or alter the profile of the aft face of any surface-drive prop, as this will alter the pitch and the cupping. If you know what you are doing, you may wish to modify these for a particular reason, but customising props is a vastly complicated

The little balancer in close-up. The shaft floats between two magnets and there is very little friction.

A homemade balancer. It is a little crude, but it works well.

subject, and experimenting on metal props can quickly become expensive.

While filing or sanding the forward face of the blade, work on the leading edge so that you get it really sharp. Take great care when sharpening and balancing a prop, otherwise you will end up with a least one deep cut on a finger.

HEALTH WARNING

Many props are made from beryllium copper (BeCu), although they may also be ordered in silicon brass, aluminium and sometimes in stainless steel. Beryllium copper dust is a health hazard and you must avoid inhaling it when working on props or wedge rudders made from this material. Avoid using power tools for sharpening as they throw a fine mist of particles into the air. When sanding, use wet and dry paper and plenty of water to damp down any dust. If you really must use a Dremel or similar (which is admittedly much quicker), use a professional dust mask and safety glasses. You should also wear gloves to avoid getting the dust in any cuts.

Use a needle file to remove all the casting flash from the prop boss, finishing with successively finer grades of wet and dry paper.

When you have a nicely balanced, sharpened prop, the last job is to run a file down the trailing edge to ensure the edges of the 'wedge' are sharp. This will allow water to break cleanly off the blades. Some people like to polish their props to a mirror finish, while others prefer to leave them in a satin finish with 1200-grit wet and dry paper. There is some confusion as to which is best from an efficiency point of view. In practice, there is no obvious difference, so it is down to individual choice. It takes time to achieve a highly polished finish on a BeCu prop and it will not stay that way for long anyway, as the material tarnishes quickly, especially when wet.

Submerged props should be finished in a similar way, but here sometimes the trailing edge is also sharpened. There are, however, some excellent CNC aluminium props available, such as those from Doctor Props, ETTI and Tenshock, that will save you the trouble.

If you do not fancy all the bother of sharpening and balancing, you can get someone else to do it for you. Model Marine Supplies, the UK Octura importer, will supply props ready sharpened and balanced at additional cost. Similarly, Prop Shop, a UK manufacturer of propellers, supplies all of its range of scale, IC and fast electric props sharpened, balanced and ready to use. Because it is a domestic company, Prop Shop's prices are very competitive in comparison with imported products.

PITCH

The quoted pitch of any prop is the theoretical distance the prop would travel forwards in one rotation. No prop is 100 per cent efficient, and all suffer from greater or lesser amounts of slippage.

If you know the pitch of the prop and have a rough idea how fast the motor can turn it, you can calculate how fast the boat is going. However, because it is impossible to know exactly how much the prop is slipping – in other words, how efficient it is – and the exact motor rpm under load, any speed figures you arrive at will be at best a good guess. The only way to know exactly how fast the boat is going is to accurately time it over a known distance or use an on-board GPS, several of which are available on the internet.

Prop pitch can be fine-tuned using a pair of pliers to tweak the blades to achieve longer run times, more lift from a hydro prop or more straight-line speed. There are so many factors involved, however, and so many different possibilities, that it is difficult to give recommendations.

Choosing the best prop for a boat can involve a lot of trial and error and expense. Asking around among other boat owners, to try to get a base-line for your search, can save time and money. However, even if you do end up with a prop that gives your boat a performance that you are happy with, is it really the best one for your boat? Could the boat go faster or longer? There are so many factors involved and sometimes you just have to make an educated guess – and working out the pitch can be the most awkward of the guessing games. There is a clear relationship between the diameter of the prop and the blade pitch; they are two factors that have to be considered (guessed at) as two parts of the same problem. Added to that, you also need to consider blade shape.

One method for calculating prop pitch is to divide the expected (hoped-for) speed of the model, in *inches* per minute, by the anticipated motor rpm. This will give the necessary actual advance of the prop in inches for one revolution. Add to this the percentage slip, estimated at around 10 to 20 per cent, and then multiply the resulting figure by 1.15, to get the geometric pitch required. Check the diameters of props that other boaters are using for the same class of boat and take an average to use with the pitch you have calculated. If the boat does not reach the expected speed, the motor may not be delivering the anticipated revs, and a reduction in diameter or blade area may improve things. Unfortunately, efficiency falls with reduction of area and/or the diameter, so a better speed might be obtained by a slightly larger prop with less pitch, especially if slip decreases.

PROBLEMS AND SOLUTIONS

You need to make sure the prop you are using matches the particular combination of motor, number of cells, and gear ratio (if applicable), as well as boat size, weight and type. If the propeller is too big, the motor will be overloaded. If the prop is too small, it will not develop enough thrust for good acceleration and top speed.

Bigger props are generally more efficient than smaller props and will provide more thrust, but will also magnify handling problems such as torque roll and prop walking. Generally speaking, always use the biggest prop you can get away with that gives you the desired duration without overloading the motor. For brief bursts of speed, for instance in a speed records boat, you can use quite a big prop, which will give you very much greater speed. Using a very large prop will make the motor draw very high current, and for this reason you should keep run times short. Most motors can cope with being overloaded for a minute or so, but if they are run in this way for much longer, they will start to seriously overheat and burn up.

If the boat will not get on to the plane, either the prop is too small or you are not turning it fast enough. In other words, you do not have enough power. If your drive system allows you to alter prop depth, try running the prop deeper. You may find the greater thrust from a bigger prop makes the hull work more efficiently, and that the boat runs faster for the same or a longer duration. However, a prop that is too big may bog the motor down and the boat will not be very quick. In that case, try a smaller prop or one with less pitch and blade area, or if possible raise the strut to bring the prop further out of the water.

Hydro props, such as the Octura 17 series, are very efficient at high speed when the boat is planing, but slip a lot at low speed and take a while to accelerate from standstill. Some props, particularly hydro props, can suffer slippage when the boat is turning due to a loss of forward speed. Hydros do not like turning too tightly, so turns should be wider and gentler to maintain forward speed. This is less of a problem on monos and tunnels using the props with less lift because of the trailing-edge cupping these props often have.

REPAIRING PROPS

If you are unlucky and damage a prop through running over debris or another boat, it is often possible to repair it, depending on the material the prop is made from and the extent of the damage. Carbon-fibre props will shatter on impact, leaving you only the boss and a few slivers of blade. Beryllium copper is quite soft and will tend to deform when struck. Using a pair of pliers, either the smooth-jawed type or a pair with the serrated faces ground smooth or covered in tape, it may be possible to carefully bend the blades back into shape. You can buy a small ball anvil for this, which can also be used for fine-tuning the blade shape by adding or removing trailing-edge cupping.

Most of the damage will usually be on the leading edge of the blades. When you have the damaged blades as accurately realigned as possible, re-sharpen and balance the prop as though it is new. A repaired prop will invariably be slightly smaller in diameter and blade area than a brand-new one, but you will have saved a useable prop that you can keep as a spare.

If you start attending race meetings on a regular basis, it is a good idea to have at least one finished spare prop of the size(s) you use most. They are expensive, but it is frustrating to travel a long way to a meeting, lose your only good prop in the first race, and have nothing to replace it. It is also worth carrying a few needle files and some wet and dry paper to repair minor damage.

STORAGE

Metal props are not cheap. A collection of more than a dozen or so represents quite an investment, so it makes sense to look after them properly. Storing them loose together in a box is asking for chipped edges and scratched faces.

Fishing-tackle boxes or any kind of multi-compartmented box that can contain props individually will work well. One example is a

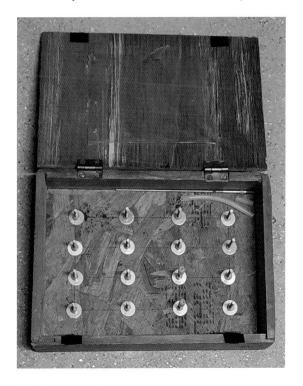

Wooden prop-storage box.

A prop box made from a sewing box bought in a supermarket.

sewing box with removable trays with various small compartments. Some even have a section designed for keeping cotton reels on tapered posts, which are ideal for props.

Alternatively, you could make a simple wooden box, with a false floor with 4mm bolts fitted through holes in it. Each prop can be retained by a small piece of silicon tube slid over the studding. This will keep each one apart from the others so the blades cannot touch together and get damaged.

Two Mini Monos battling it out in some very rough conditions for these small boats.

Chapter Eight

Rechargeable Cells

The battery pack is probably the most important and least understood component in any fast electric model boat. This is the device that ultimately makes a fast electric go, and the way it performs directly determines the performance of the whole boat. Without a basic understanding of cells and how to look after them, it is impossible to achieve the best speed and duration. Even if the motor, speed controller, drive system and boat design are of the highest quality, they can do nothing without a good battery.

The way cells were supplied in the past – in loose matched items that had to be made into packs.

TERMINOLOGY: BATTERIES AND CELLS

It is easy to confuse the terms relating to battery power. Rechargeable cells are referred to here – it may seem pedantic, but there is a good reason for this. For example, an AA 'battery' is not, despite what it says on the pack, a battery. It is a single cell. However, four AA cells in series make up a 6-volt battery. Batteries are made up of several cells wired together, no matter what construction or chemistry they are. (As an aside, PP3 9-volt batteries are actually batteries. Despite their appearance, they are constructed from six 1.5-volt cells.)

Sometimes, a battery may be referred to as a battery pack or cell pack. This is because racers, pre-LiPos, used to buy separate cells that had to be soldered together by the purchaser. Battery retailers would buy the cells by the thousand, graded and computer-matched, and sell 'packs' of them in a box. There were usually six or seven in each box, with labels on them, so that the purchaser could see how closely matched they were. They were just boxes of cells until the buyer soldered them together, when they became a battery. It became the norm to use the term 'cell pack' to describe a made-up battery.

Random cells left over from pack building. They have never been used and are now useless. The scales show the relative weights of a 7.2 NiMh pack and a 7.4-volt LiPo battery.

LiPos are much lighter for about the same capacity.

NICADs AND NIMHs

In the 1980s and 1990s, everyone involved with racing boats used Sub C-sized nickel cadmium (NiCad) cells, which were rated at 1.2 volts per cell. They are very rarely seen these days. In the past, all manufacturers of rechargeable cells would try to increase the capacity of the cells to give more run time or more speed. This was fine at first, but over time the cells became very weak and liable to fail quickly, after one run in some cases. In the nick of time, the manufacturers introduced the nickel metal hydride (NiMh) cell, on show at the 1999 World Championships. At first, they were an improvement on the NiCad cells (but still 1.2 volt per cell), but then the arms race began again, with the same result: high-capacity cells that were weak and liable to fail quickly. Not only was this annoying, it was also quite costly. Although it was possible to buy cheaper, pre-made 'sport' packs, for numerous reasons they were not suitable for high-level racing. As an example, racers in the late 1990s were paying £10 to £12 per cell for well-matched ones. If, for example, they were running in a twelve-cell class, it was costing £120 to £144 per cell pack – and a pack was needed for each heat (usually three per meeting).

NiMh cells would take a day or so to recover fully after a race. Although they could be recharged safely during a race meeting, they would only reach around 80 per cent charge and that would not win a race.

Various labels with all matching data printed for each cell.

NiCad cells, with the jig that is used for soldering cells together.

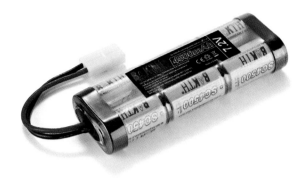

A commercial ready-made 7.2-volt NiMh battery pack.

LITHIUM POLYMER CELLS (LIPO)

NiMh cells certainly had their limitations and when lithium polymer (LiPo) cells began to appear, they were a huge improvement in terms of performance and price. An arms race did begin again, but this time a device was developed that negates (at least for the time being) the greater capacity, more costly, very fragile 'arms-race' cells. This device will be explained fully at the end of the chapter. Made up NiMh 'sport' packs are still available at a reasonable price for those who are not interested in racing, but LiPos will always be preferable to NiMh cells.

Unfortunately, in the past, LiPo cells have had a bad reputation in terms of safety, exhibiting a tendency to catch fire. LiPos will not usually explode but the fires, if they happen, are quick and intense. The current crop of LiPos are much more stable than the early ones. As long as the cells are looked after and the safety recommendations are followed, there should not be any problems. The reason why there were a number of fires in the early days was probably because people did not know the best way to handle the cells. LiPo fires were almost always the fault of the user, sometimes leaving the battery on a higher charge than was recommended, going off to do something else and forgetting about it. To be fair, most types of cell would have the same reaction after suffering that type of abuse. Indeed, NiMh

cells could sometimes even explode, although this was thankfully a rare occurrence.

Undoubtedly, the LiPo cells are a huge step forward and the advantages over NiMh cells are irrefutable. For a start, the power to weight ratio is much better, as LiPo cells are quite a bit lighter and can store at least the same or more energy in relation to their capacity when compared with NiMh cells. The level of power output remains steady throughout the discharge time, whereas the output of NiMh cells starts to decrease very soon after charging. The NiMh discharge curve shows a marked reduction in output availability while the LiPo has a much flatter discharge curve.

A bit more up to date: four packs of LiPos, the first three from the top down are all 2S, while the bottom one is 2S2P. The different sizes of packs all have the same voltage but different capacity.

A new Zippy compact 2S pack, with all the necessary information printed on the label: voltage, C rating, mAh capacity and even the watt/hour rating. It would also be useful to know the IR of cells as supplied.

A hard-case battery of the type more often used in RC cars. With great care, the plastic case can be split open and the battery removed to save weight. That is the plan for this one.

This means that, with similar rated capacities, the LiPo will give a better performance and a longer run time and be lighter in weight. As an added bonus, LiPos have a very low self-discharge rate. In practice, this means that, if the cells are charged but not used, they will still be more or less fully charged a week later.

When LiPos were introduced, all the racing classes had to be changed. This was because the nominal voltage of a LiPo cell is 3.7 volts as opposed to 1.2 volts for NiMhs (and NiCads). This meant that, for example, a seven-cell NiMh class would be 8.4 volts. There was no direct or close equivalent – a two-cell LiPo would be 7.4 volts and a three-cell would be 11.1 volts. The twelve-cell (14.4v) classes would be closest at 14.8 volts with a four-cell LiPo battery. As a result, eventually all the classes were changed to work with the new cells (*see* Chapter 13).

VOLTAGE AND CELL COUNT

It is not vital to have a deep understanding of the chemistry of cells in order to get the best out of them, but some basic knowledge can be useful. The nominal (average) voltage of a LiPo cell is deemed to be 3.7 volts and all boat classes assume

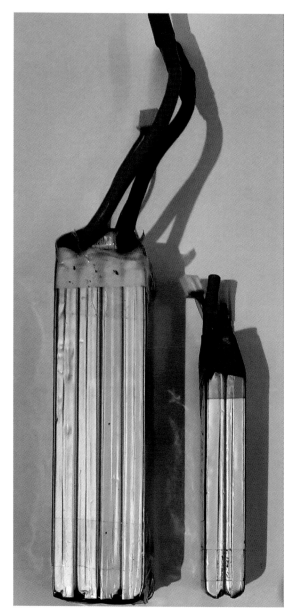

Strange as it may seem, these are both 7.4-volt batteries: (right) 2S and (left) 2S2P.

Different pack architecture: the rear battery has four cells but is only 7.4 volts (2S2P), while the one at the front has four cells but is 14.8 volts (4S). The main reason for showing this is because the front battery has puffed up. If this happens, even if it is only one cell, the battery must not be used and should be disposed of safely.

this value to be universal. In fact, a good-quality fully charged LiPo cell is at 4.2v, and sometimes 4.23v if it is very good. The lowest you should ever discharge a LiPo to is 3.0v. That is the absolute lower limit – below this, damage will probably occur. Assuming a full charge, a LiPo cell will be at 4.2v, which will then quite quickly drop under load to about 3.7v for the majority of the run. Once the voltage drops to around 3.4v, it is to all intents and purposes flat and will give very little usable performance. Ideally, the ESC will have a low voltage cut-off (LVC). Many are set at 3 volts, but it is preferable to have it at 3.2 volts, if the setting can be reprogrammed. Many of the cheaper ESCs have no LVC at all, so they are to be avoided at all costs.

A LiPo cell has a nominal voltage of 3.7v. A two-cell battery (2S, or two cells in series) will be made up of two cells wired in series, positive to negative. When wired in series, the voltages are added together to give 7.4 volts. As 2S means two cells in series, it follows that 3S means three cells in series (11.1v), 4S means 14.8 volts, and so on.

CAPACITY AND INTERNAL RESISTANCE

Sometimes, batteries are sold as '2S2P'. This means two 2S batteries wired together in parallel.

Wiring batteries in parallel means that the capacity of the battery is doubled, but the voltage remains the same. As an example, a 2S2P 2200mAh battery would still be 7.4v but the capacity would be 4400mAh.

The capacity of a battery is basically a measure of how much power it can hold, stated in milliamp hours (mAh). For example, a battery with a 5000mAh capacity can support a discharge of 5 amps (1000mAh = 1Ah) for one hour, 10 amps for 30 minutes, 20 amps for 15 minutes, and so on. In practice, however, none of this is going to happen – as soon as a load is applied to that 5000mAh battery, its actual capacity is going to reduce. To make matters worse, the capacity will reduce in proportion to the size of the load. However, assuming the battery manufacturer or reseller is being accurate and honest, the stated capacity is a reasonable guide.

The other part of the capacity figure is the charging rate. This is related to the capacity, so a 5000mAh battery (5 amp) should be charged at 5 amps. Some suppliers claim that their batteries can be charged at three or four times the capacity rating, but this should be ignored. Sticking to the capacity rating will give you the best and safest charge and help the battery to last longer.

There is another 'C rating' to be aware of: a measure of how much current the battery can safely provide on a continuous basis. It is arrived at by multiplying the capacity (5000mAh in the example) by the 'C' number printed on the label attached to the battery. It could be 25C, 40C or 60C, up to 100C plus. If it is 60C, the calculation would be 60C x 5 amps = 300 amps, indicating that 300 amps is the maximum safe continuous current that the battery will supply. Like so many others, this is a theoretical figure and will not hold up in the real world. As soon as the battery is under load, the actual capacity will reduce and the calculation will go out of the window.

Sometimes, there will be two C ratings on a battery label. One is the normal rating, while the other (the higher one) is a 'burst' rating. The burst will allow for perhaps twenty to thirty seconds at that higher rate.

Unfortunately, manufacturers are sometimes a bit 'liberal' when it comes to rating their batteries. It is not unheard of for the quoted C rating of a pack to actually be the burst rating. The likely result is that the pack will destroy itself when operated continuously at a rate that is, in effect, much higher than the rate it can handle.

Batteries will experience a reduction in capacity and voltage under heavy load and a battery with a higher C rating will give greater 'headroom'. For example, a 20C 5000mAh battery should (in theory) provide a constant 100-amp discharge, but in practice, it will probably be less than that. If a motor draws 40 amps, that is 40 per cent of the theoretical maximum the battery will support. Using a 40C 5000mAh battery, the same motor would only draw 20 per cent of the maximum and there would therefore be less stress on the battery than on the previous example. This means that the battery would be able to maintain the 40-amp discharge for a longer period, but given a fixed running time the battery should perform well over that period and its service life will be longer. This is the basic premise behind the design and use of energy limiters.

When selecting the right C rating for a battery you will need to consider the power draw of the motor. More may equal better in terms of the battery's life, but a higher C-rated battery will not necessarily make a boat faster. There is, though, a tenuous correlation between the C rating of a battery and its internal resistance. A battery with a higher C rating will usually have a lower internal resistance (IR). This is not always the case, because there are inevitably variables in the manufacturing process, but in general it seems to hold true and, all else being equal, a pack with lower IR will allow a model to go a little faster. This is because, simply put, the lower the resistance, the less restriction the battery encounters

in delivering the required power. It is really the IR that makes a battery perform more efficiently, not the C rating. It is also interesting to note that some of the newer batteries on the market are including the WHr (watt/hour) equivalent of the C rating on the label (*see* Chapter 9, on energy limiters).

OHM'S LAW

There is one important detail that is omitted when people talk about buying a LiPo battery: the manufacturers do not print the IR on the label. This is because the internal resistance of a battery will change over time, sometimes because of the temperature of the cells. As resistance is involved, the calculations relate to Ohm's Law.

Ohm's Law says that the current (amps) through a conductor between two points is directly proportional to the difference in voltage across those two points. Simply put, amps = volts/resistance, so, the higher the internal resistance in a cell, the less current it can provide and the lower the output voltage will be. Although it is possible to race successfully without ever knowing the IR of the battery, it is important to be aware of it, because it is a good indicator of the health of the battery. It will be even better if you can calculate the individual cell resistances.

Anything under 10mΩ per cell is great cell condition and 10mΩ to 15mΩ is fine, while 15mΩ to 20mΩ is bit old; it is probably best to use the latter for practice or fun running. Anything over 20mΩ indicates that it is time to retire the battery, but if the cells are in good physical condition they could perhaps be used in a scale boat that draws less current than a race boat.

Because IR has such an important role in efficiency, it is useful to be able to calculate it. Some battery chargers on the market include an IR testing function, most of which will give individual

When a LiPo battery destroys itself: a composite time lapse of a battery catching fire. From the beginning of the event to the fireball on the right took just over a minute. Luckily, this is rare, but it is a reminder that good safety policies are vital when using LiPos.

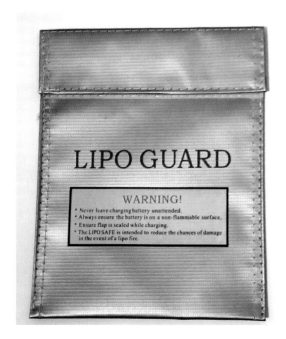

Strictly speaking, LiPos should be stored and carried in a sealed metal case, and charged in one as well. At race events, however, most competitors do not bother, because there are plenty of people around who would be able to deal with a fire. Although such incidents are extremely rare, it is important to be aware of what can happen.

cell values. Some will give only the pack IR, but even that is useful as an alert for a failing battery. There is a way to check IR if the charger does not have that function but it can be fiddly and involves other equipment, such as a watt meter, a resistive load or possibly a good quality multi-meter. There are videos online of the several different procedures. A stand-alone IR checker would be a good piece of kit to have.

If you are able to test IR, it is advisable to do this on any new cells as soon as you get them and record the figures. After that initial test, keep testing the cells regularly and keep recording the results. This will help you to spot signs of the battery starting to age.

There is nothing to fear from LiPo batteries, as long as you follow the guidelines and treat them with the respect they deserve. Finally, if you are going to be storing batteries for more than a couple of weeks, storing charge to around 3.8v per cell will keep them in good condition. Almost all good chargers will have a storage charge facility and will automatically charge up to that voltage, or discharge down to that voltage.

SAFETY: LIPO BATTERIES

MPBA-FES Guidance for Use and Care of LiPos

This official guidance is taken directly from the Model Power Boat Association Fast Electric Section (MPBA-FES) website (with thanks to the writer Martin Marriott for permission to reproduce it).

LiPo batteries are now used by a very significant number of model boaters and they must be treated differently to more conventional rechargeable batteries.

The most useful aspect of their operation is the very low self-discharge rate, which can be as low as one or two per cent per month. This gives them the extremely useful property of being able to be charged when you come home from boating and still be fresh and ready to use even several weeks later. Anyone who has forgotten to put their batteries on charge the night before a boating session will appreciate that. However, they are different to conventional cells and probably the most important aspect of these batteries from a safety point of view are the consequences of overcharging, over discharging and crash damage.

The individual Li-Po cells are nominally 3.7 volts with a maximum fully charged rating of 4.23 volts and a minimum safe discharged rating of 3 volts. If you over discharge the battery too much below 3 volts per cell you will almost certainly damage it permanently and it will not then accept a re-charge. NEVER leave a Li-Po battery connected to something that will allow even the slightest discharge, as the battery will be effectively destroyed in a few hours.

If you charge your battery beyond the 4.23 volt per cell limit, you risk damaging the battery and also have the possibility of a thermal runaway, resulting in a battery fire. You MUST use a dedicated Li-Po charger and, if your charger is not automatic, you MUST make sure that the voltage control on the charger is set correctly for the number of cells in the battery you are charging.

Most Li-Po cells and chargers have a cell balancing facility and the use of this will help keep the cells working efficiently and safely. In fact, we would not recommend the purchase of a Li-Po charger that didn't have this facility available.

You must also use a speed controller (ESC) that is designed for use with Li-Pos and will not allow them to over-discharge.

Other precautions should also be taken when charging.

Do not charge at more than 1C unless specifically authorised by the pack vendor.

Never charge batteries in a model, always remove them from the model.

Charge on a safe surface in a position where a battery flare cannot ignite other items.

A Li-Po burn only lasts a few seconds so it is not a long-term fire source, but it is extremely hot and will easily ignite other flammable items that are in close proximity. Dedicated 'charging bags' are also available that will contain any Li-Po flare if used correctly.

Damaged cells are usually very easy to spot as they 'balloon' out.

The cells are generally 'softer' than the traditional Ni-Cd types and are much more susceptible to crash damage. Any visible damage to the cell should be treated with suspicion.

Any cell that is 'ballooned' by charge/discharge problems or by crash damage should be discarded.

Any cells you wish to discard must be made safe. The commonest recommended method of doing this with a damaged cell is to discharge the cell electrically and then submerge it in strong salt water for at least 12 hours. After this the cell is inert and may be disposed of at your local recycling site. For more guidance on the subject you should consult the Internet for the latest information on cell disposal.

Always read the manufacturer's information on the cells you are using, as this will give you the information on maximum charge and discharge rates.

Checking LiPo volts in cells
  4.23v = 100%
  4.03v = 76%
  3.86v = 52%
  3.83v = 42% = typically used as a storage charge Recommended
  3.80v = 30%
  3.75v = 11%
  3.70v = 0%

(These are resting voltages, not under-load voltages.)

All models must have a kill switch for the radio-control equipment (excluding scale craft) that is operated from the outside of the model (loop system is recommended). In case of emergency the competitor, start assistant, recovery boat or any other person can interrupt the power supply between the motor and batteries.
  Recommended for the race platform or pits area: a first aid kit, fire extinguisher, fire blanket and a bucket of dry sand has to be present. It is up to the officer of the day to see where these are allocated on the day.

Lithium Metal Fires
Lithium metal fires must be tackled with a specialist lithium extinguisher, commonly sold as an L2 extinguisher. A sodium chloride extinguisher is not suitable for use on a lithium metal fire. Cells/batteries not containing lithium as a pure metal do not require an L2 extinguisher.
  DO NOT USE A WATER EXTINGUISHER
  If any fire gets out of hand call 999.
  MPBA members are expected to operate LiPo cells in a safe and responsible manner.
  Batteries shall be securely fixed in the boat.
  Do not mix batteries from different manufacturers.
  The following changes are allowed across the board for all classes of competition i.e. Fast Electric, Scale, Round the Pole Hydroplanes and Straight Running, whether it be for physical problems of getting cells into a boat or for class weight restrictions.

1. Removal of the plastic covering to enable batteries to comply with the required weight limits or physical problems of getting cells into a boat is permitted.
2. Competitors are able to change the connectors if they wish.
3. The wires can be changed as long as they are capable of taking the expected current load.
4. Please make sure that all other terminals apart from the one you are working on are covered with an insulating material to avoid the possibility of a short circuit. On completion of alterations please ensure that all connectors are insulated and that all bare cell terminals are covered with polyimide tape or another suitable heatproof material (fibreglass tape is also suitable). This will ensure that there will not be a short circuit from any wires including balance leads.
5. NEVER ALTER THE GREY/SILVER PLASTIC CELL SACKS IN ANY WAY

  These measures should only be carried out by competent people. If in any doubt as to your own ability you should take advice from someone who has the required experience. Sometimes balance leads break away from a cell tag due to fatigue. The cell connection therefore has to be repaired or the battery thrown away. The latter is not an economic solution so it will be necessary to take the above precautions to re-solder the wire.

  There is nothing to fear from LiPo batteries, as long as you follow the guidelines and treat them with the respect they deserve. Finally, if you are going to be storing batteries for more than a couple of weeks, storing charge to around 3.8v per cell will keep them in good condition. Almost all good chargers will have a storage charge facility and will automatically charge up to that voltage, or discharge down to that voltage.

Chapter Nine

Battery Chargers and Energy Limiters

CHOOSING A CHARGER

Most modern chargers are very comprehensive and will charge virtually all types of rechargeable battery that are likely to be used in a boat, including of course NiMh cells and LiPos. The first piece of advice is do not go cheap. Really cheap chargers are a total waste of money. But that does not mean you have to spend a fortune either. Ask around other club members to find out what they are using to charge their LiPos. There will usually be someone who has an interest in fast electrics. Many scale boaters are also using LiPos and will have good chargers.

A very smart dual-channel charger with an excellent display showing all the relevant information about the battery's state, including cell IR.

A single-output 20-amp charger that will charge LiPos, NiCad/NiMh cells and sealed lead-acid batteries. The charger can charge up to 6 LiPos at up to 20 amps.

The Graupner Polaron charger, another very comprehensive dual-channel charger with its accompanying power supply.

Look for a charger that will charge LiPo batteries from 1 to 6S with a charge rate of up to 10 amps at least. All good-quality units will be able to charge different types of battery, including LiPos and Li-ions, and will allow you to set parameters such as charging current, cell count, end voltage, and so on. All programmable chargers will have a screen that shows information such as the charging progress, voltage of the battery, and the current that is going into the battery. They will also allow for discharging and storage charging capabilities.

Some chargers will measure the overall internal resistance of the battery. This may not be very precise, but it can still be useful for monitoring the health of the batteries over a period of time.

Functions and Modes

Although most chargers will have several useful and often programmable functions, the three you will need the most are balance charge, discharge and storage charge. The one mode that should not be used unless you are charging NiMh cells is 'fast charge'. This mode does what its name suggests, but it does not balance the cells in the pack, which is not a good idea with LiPos. 'Balance' mode is always the best and safest way of charging LiPo batteries. You have to plug in both the main lead and the balance lead, so the charger can read the voltages of all the cells and can then automatically balance the cells during charging to avoid problems.

Two well-used chargers with identical functionality. The main difference is that the left-hand one has a touch screen, which is more convenient than having to scroll through the options using buttons. Both chargers can read individual cell IR.

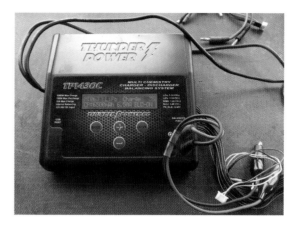

Another powerful single-channel charger, which can charge at up to 30 amps.

While it is generally not a good idea to buy cheap, these two chargers were only about £30 each. These particular items are no longer available, but there are numerous chargers on sale that are identical in all but name.

The storage charge mode is also important as LiPos should be left at storage voltage when not in use for a while.

Number of Outputs/Channels

Most chargers are single-output, which means only one battery can be charged at a time. A charger with more than one output can charge several batteries at the same time. As each output acts as a self-contained charger, it is possible to charge different batteries regardless of their capacity, voltage level, cell count and even different cell types. This type of charger is more expensive, but it is also more flexible, and will make charging faster if you have different types of batteries.

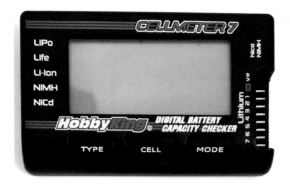

Two identical Schulte dual-channel chargers being powered from a single dual-channel power supply.

Two versions of a piece of kit all RC boaters should have. They plug into the balance leads on a LiPo and will read the capacity left in the cells after a run. The smaller one can have a voltage level pre-set and the buzzers will sound and the LED will flash. They are mainly used in RC aircraft but could be handy in a boat when operating alone.

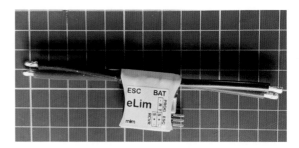

The eLim, a UK-made limiter to comply with NAVIGA and MPBA racing rules.

Similar to the previous cell meter, this piece of equipment can also read the individual cell internal resistance. This is handy if your charger does not have that facility.

Power Supply

Some chargers have a built-in power supply that allows them to be powered directly from an AC wall socket and some have the facility to be powered by mains or battery. However, the majority of LiPo

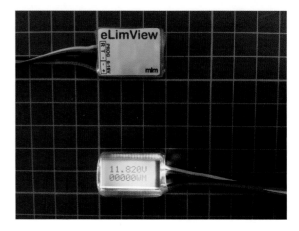

A companion to the eLim, which turns the eLim into an energy meter, a voltmeter and an ammeter.

chargers are designed for a 12-volt power supply, such as a car battery. If you want to be able to charge one of these easily in the workshop you will have to purchase an external power supply (PSU) that will provide the correct voltage when under load. The rated output of the PSU should be well above the power demand of the charger if you want to get the most out of it. For example, if you have a 100W charger, you will need a power supply that is rated higher than 100W. The more 'headroom' there is, the less likely it is that the charger will be damaged. It will also allow you to use the same PSU if you acquire a more powerful charger in the future.

ENERGY LIMITERS

(Article taken from the MPBA-FES website, reproduced with kind permission from its author Martin Marriott, designer and manufacturer of the eLim energy limiter.)

History
Back in 2015/16, in fast electric model boat racing to NAVIGA/MPBA rules, the problem of poor LiPo battery life had become a major problem.

The rules limit the battery weight to 560g for the Mono 2 and Hydro 2 classes, 280g for the Mono 1, Hydro 1 and Eco Expert classes and 110g for the Mini classes. The quest for ever greater performance leads to competitors pushing the LiPo packs to their limits by charging to maximum voltage (4.23V), discharging to or below their minimum voltage (3.0V) and drawing very high currents from them.

At the same time, manufacturers produced packs with ever higher capacities but they have become less robust with lower C ratings.

The result is that the life of packs can be very short and as the cost is high (>£50 per pack) the cost of racing has become a concern as it was felt that some modellers were leaving the hobby due to the high costs.

Also, despite what it may say on the label, not all batteries deliver their rated capacity and if they do, they don't do it for long. This means that not all racers are competing with the same amount of energy.

The governing body (NAVIGA) therefore investigated alternative methods of avoiding overstressing the LiPo packs so that much greater life can be achieved. One method that they investigated was the use of energy limiters. Energy meters were also investigated but were discounted.

The design brief was to produce a device that was small, accurate and relatively low cost. Discussion took place as to what should happen when the allocated amount of energy had been consumed and it was decided that it should reduce the speed of the boat gradually to zero and that it should remain disabled for a period of time before re-enabling.

Alternative designs were produced by three suppliers which were extensively field tested during 2016/17. Much debate occurred within the racing community but at the NAVIGA Presidium in August 2017, the vote was taken to allow the use of limiters alongside the existing NAVIGA rules batteries. The decision on energy levels and other rules was deferred to allow feedback from all country leaders.

Based on this feedback, a questionnaire was issued in November 2017 which had a deadline of the end of November. Of the 21 countries eligible to vote, 15 responded with the following result:

Energy Limits
Mini Classes – 20 WattHr
Eco, Mono 1, Hydro 1 – 58 WattHr
Mono 2, Hydro 2 – 116 WattHr
FSRE – 174 WattHr
Frequency of update to limit – Once a year
Calibration in the field – No

Set a Min or Max battery weight – No
Ramp-down time – 5 secs
Dead time – 60 secs
Check voltage before race – Yes
Check voltage after race – Yes
Do we accept the current types of limiter – Yes
Do we accept new types – Yes
These decisions will be incorporated into the NAVIGA rules from 1st Jan 2018.

What does an energy limiter do?

The energy limiter is an electronic device which is placed between the battery and the rest of the boat electronics (ESC, motor, Rx, etc.). It is also connected between the receiver throttle output and the ESC input. The limiter constantly monitors the instantaneous voltage and current so that the power (watts) can be calculated.

This is logged over time to determine how much energy has been consumed (WattHrs).

The limiter is pre-programmed with the amount of energy that the boat will be allowed to use in the race. When this is consumed, the maximum throttle signal that is passed to the ESC will ramp down from the maximum to zero over a period of time. At the time of writing, this is 5 seconds. The limiter will keep the throttle demand to zero for the 'dead time'. This is currently 60 seconds. After this time, the throttle restriction is removed so that the racer can return to the pontoon.

How does an energy limiter help?

The limiter is connected to a larger more robust battery but only allows a pre-determined amount of energy to be used. Because the battery is not fully discharged, it will now last much longer and will now deliver exactly the same amount of energy each time to all competitors.

How does energy (WattHr) relate to capacity (AmpHr)?

Racers are familiar with battery capacity which is printed on the label of all LiPos, for instance 5000mAh (ie 5 AmpHr). This means that it could deliver 5 amps for 1 hour.

Now this is not the same as energy. Clearly, a 2S 5 AmpHr battery doesn't contain as much energy as a 3S 5 AmpHr battery. All that is required to calculate the energy in the battery is to multiply the AmpHr number by the nominal battery voltage. Therefore a 3S 5 AmpHr battery contains 3 x 3.7V x 5 AmpHr = 55.5 WattHr (if we assume the cell nominal voltage is 3.7 volts).

Using this formula, the following table shows some approximate equivalence for the 2019 limits.

One of the major benefits of a limiter is that battery life can be much improved. In order to ensure this, the battery must have a capacity which exceeds that used, by a reasonable amount. 120% is a good starting point but will of course need to be modified depending upon what batteries are available.

Suggested Capacities for use with Limiters

WattHr (WattMins)	AmpHr (3S)	x1.2 AHr (3S)	AmpHr (2S)	x1.2 AHr (2S)	Comment
21 (1260)	1.892	2.270	2.838	3.406	Mini classes (NADs/MPBA/NAVIGA)
60 (3600)	5.405	6.486	8.108	9.730	M1/H1 classes (NADs/MPBA/NAVIGA)

Energy Limits

The table below shows the energy levels approved as of 2020 for the various organisations and clubs.

Band	NAVIGA	MPBA-FES	NADs
1-(MM/MH)	21(1260)	21(1260)	21(1260)
2-(M1/H1/Eco)	60(3600)	60(3600)	60(3600)
3-(M2/H2/CAT)	120(7200)	120(7200)	120(7200)
4-(FSRE)	180(10800)	180(10800)	180(10800)

Note: Values shown are WattHrs (WattMins)

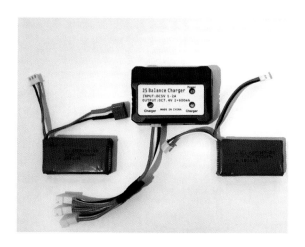

A 'toy' RC boat bought online might come with a charger and LiPo batteries, but this type of charging set-up is not ideal. The batteries are charged through the balance leads instead of the actual battery leads and, despite what the little USB-powered charger box says, the battery is not being correctly balanced. The left battery shows that changing the plug on the two-wire lead allows you to use a 'proper' LiPo charger and plug the other lead into the balance port of the charger.

To summarise, the two main points for keeping cells in good condition are:
1. Do not leave your batteries at full charge for extended periods.
2. Do not leave them in a low state of charge. After a day's racing, always put them into storage mode as soon as possible.

Chapter Ten

Radio Control

Radio-control technology has been around for a long time, although it seems as if in the past it was most often used for military purposes. It was not until after World War II that it started to become usable by hobbyists. These days, good RC systems can be affordable and generally very reliable.

A boat needs only a simple two-channel radio, but it must be of reasonable quality and installed properly to ensure reliable operation. Failure of the radio system in a scale boat or yacht is unlikely to be hugely dramatic, but any loss of control of a fast electric boat doing 40+mph may lead to its owner going home with a bag of bits. It may also cause serious damage to anything in its way. My own experience of watching my 4S cat destroy itself against a concrete wall due to a radio fault is not to be recommended!

Modern radio systems, even the cheaper sets, are usually quite reliable and will tolerate surprising amounts of misuse. Most of my own radio gear has been wet more than once, yet continues to function perfectly when dried out. Obviously, it is advisable to waterproof everything as much and as carefully as possible. The receiver (RX) can, for example, be placed in a balloon sealed by tie-wraps. Many ESCs are at least splash-proof, and it is possible to buy waterproof servos. Non-waterproof servos can be protected from splashes by sealing all the joints in the case, as well as the control wire exit.

If you cannot avoid using your model in the rain, cover the transmitter (TX) with a plastic bag. You do not really need to look at the TX during operation and this is a good cheap way of keeping it dry.

Systems include the original direct sequence spread spectrum (DSSS), which is still used today, and frequency hopping spread spectrum (FHSS) although a number of manufacturers call it AFHDS (automatic frequency hopping digital system). Simply put, the DSSS system has the receiver and

The Staveley Analogue three-channel proportional set, the same model as my first one, with its sizeable receiver and servos. The black servos are dual rotary and linear outputs.

The Furaba 27 AM Attack RC combo. This is how RC gear used to be bought, complete with matching RX and servos and all that was needed, apart from batteries. One crystal pair was also supplied. The Attack transmitter was also available in 40 MHz FM.

Two identical 2.4GHz pistol-type transmitters with different manufacturers' names: (left) one from FlySky and (right) one from Hobbyking. Both are very reliable and never cause problems.

transmitter working within a fixed section of the 2.4GHz spectrum and ignoring everything else, while FHSS (or AFHDS) works by having the TX and RX changing their operating frequency constantly within the spread of the 2.4GHz band.

FREQUENCIES

Back before the introduction of current 2.4GHz radio sets, hobbyists used 27MHz AM radios. These had two crystals to provide frequency control – one for the TX and one for the RX. These were identified mainly by colour rather than by frequency, with little coloured tabs attached to the crystals. Both TX and RX crystals needed tabs of the same colour for the system to work, and the user had to fly an appropriately coloured flag on the aerial (all 2 feet or so of it), so that others could see what frequency they were on. The reason for this was because two radios on the same frequency could

The FS-3B three-channel receiver, which works equally well with both GT2 units.

not be operated in close proximity, as there would be mutual interference. The two models could not therefore be operated at all, let alone safely.

The main frequencies and associated colour codes were as follows:

26.995MHz–26995kHz Brown or 27MHz RC Channel 1
27.045MHz–27045kHz Red or 27MHz RC Channel 2

The FS-3B, another one of my TXs (transmitters) from FlySky. This one is a three-channel 2.4GHz computer set with multiple model memories and digital control of the system set-up.

A Code RC two-channel TX, a newer and more modern-looking version of the GT2 sets.

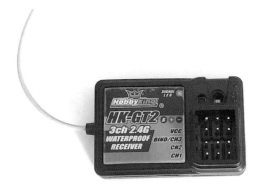

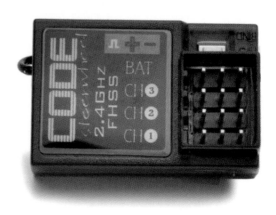

The Hobbyking three-channel RX for the GT2 TX., which works equally well with both the Hobbyking GT2 and the FlySky version, and also the FlySky three-channel TX.

The three-channel RX for the Code set.

27.095MHz–27095kHz Orange or 27MHz RC Channel 3
27.145MHz–27145kHz Yellow or 27MHz RC Channel 4
27.195MHz–27195kHz Green or 27MHz RC Channel 5
27.255MHz–27255kHz Blue or 27MHz RC Channel 6

Originally, there were only six main frequencies, known as solid colours, available. A little later, 'split' frequencies – frequencies shoehorned in between the main ones – became available. Obviously, this led to more frequencies, but it also often created more interference problems, exacerbated by the fact that CB radio used parts of the 27MHz AM band. When frequency modulation (FM) as opposed to

A more upmarket (and expensive) multi-channel stick set: the Spektrum DX6, designed for aircraft but used by smart boaters.

The FrSKY X20 Tandem TX is an aircraft unit, and expensive. It can operate on both 2.4GHz and 900MHz and the attached screen means telemetry can clearly be seen. This one might need a helicopter pilot's licence to use it!

A smart four-channel set from Futaba, with telemetry functions. It comes with a telemetry receiver, but the telemetry sensors are sold separately.

The Oxidean Marine Quasar radio boasts nine channels, a touch screen and forty model memories, and comes with a receiver and a waterproof GPS. The screen will display all the telemetry you could ever need to run a boat, including speed, and the final trick up its sleeve is that it can talk to its owner!

the original amplitude modulation (AM) was introduced, there was a small improvement, then the band was shifted to 40MHz using FM. This led to further improvement again, bringing more channels to work with, but still with crystal frequency selection. Numbers rather than colours were used to identify the frequency being used. These were basically the last three digits of the frequency, so for example 805 was the frequency 40.805MHz. Surface models such as cars and boats used 27 and 40MHz, while RC aircraft had their own band at 35MHz.

The most significant development in the story was 2.4GHz, which overnight solved most of the interference problems and gave the option for more people to run RC models in close proximity to each other.

INSTALLATION

The main problem in the past with brushed motor installations was the electrical 'noise' radiated by the motor and speed controller, which could cause interference. Motors had to be fitted with suppression capacitors and the owner had to try to keep the receiver, the aerial wire and the servo and speed controller signal wires as far from the motor, speed controller, cell pack and any power-carrying cables as possible, to reduce the possibility of interference to a minimum. This is no longer really a problem with brushless motors and 2.4MHz radio gear. However, it is still advisable to be sensible with cable runs, and so on, as there are still odd occasions where interference can occur.

Try to install everything so that it is easy to remove. If the boat gets filled with water, you will need to take everything out of it. If fitted, remove the balloon from the receiver (RX) and dry it all off. A small hairdryer is invaluable when away from home, for example at a race meeting, as is a small 12-volt ceramic heater for venues without mains power. Be warned: even a small hairdryer can melt plastic, so be careful not to heat for too long or too close to the bit you are trying to dry.

SERVOS

Once upon a time when you bought RC equipment, it came in a box with all the items needed to use it, including servos. For example, a four-channel set would usually have two or three servos and a two-channel usually only one, or (if you were lucky) possibly both. These days, it is usually a TX and RX only. This probably makes sense – there are so many different types of servo available, it is best to leave it to the buyer to choose their own. The standard-size servo that used to come with the average radio set is still perfectly adequate for most fast electric boats. Heavy, high-speed boats that have significant steering loads may benefit from using a high-output, ball-raced, metal-geared servo. Mini-or even micro-servos can be suitable for small models such as those used in Mini Hydro and Mini Mono classes, with 2S or 3S batteries, and for larger records boats as they do not really need to turn much and certainly not at speed! However, a mini

The venerable standard Futaba servo works with most radios and can be used in every kind of boat you can think of.

servo would really struggle in a 6S Mono 2 boat. In general, more expensive high-quality servos generally have higher torque output and speed and are available in a number of different speeds and sizes.

Servos usually have a three-wire ribbon lead. The most common colour code is black (0 volts), red (+5 volts) and white (signal), with the red positive wire being the central one. Some servos have a different colour code. Red is still +V and in the centre of the ribbon, but the black 0-volt lead is replaced by brown and the white signal lead is replaced by orange.

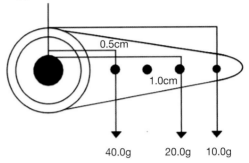

Servo arm push/pull force.

One of my spare micro servos, used as a rudder servo in the Mini Mono and in some of my small scale boats.

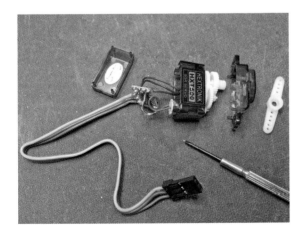

A disassembled micro servo showing the gearing and the circuit board.

Any servo, no matter how expensive or sophisticated, is only as good as its mounting and linkage. Sloppy mounting and flexible linkages will not allow the full range of servo movement, leading to slow, often imprecise steering. The only truly acceptable method of mounting a servo is to bolt it to hardwood blocks or to a proper aluminium mount.

The rudder servo should be fitted so that it is 'pulling' the rudder in the major direction of turn (right on oval racers). This is especially important on surface-drive models. There is considerable side force on the rudder in a turn and, if the servo is 'pushing' rather than 'pulling', that could cause juddering as the servo hunts for position against the force of the water on the rudder. Fitting it in this way is not always possible, however. Sometimes, this is due to the design of the stern of the boat, especially on cats, while on some other hull types the space for servo mounting is limited.

It is worth buying the strongest servo you can afford, partly because of a little-known issue that concerns the servo arm and, to an extent, the control arm fitted to the rudder. Most people know that if, when setting up the rudder, you use the outer hole in the servo arm, the pushrod and therefore the rudder will have quite a large amount of travel, but the movement will be relatively slow. If, however, you use the innermost hole in the servo arm, the movement will be faster but the rudder will have less travel. People are less aware of the fact that servos have a rated stall torque. Unfortunately,

Another essential piece of kit, a servo tester can test all aspects of the servo's movement and can even be used to test ESCs, all without using the RC system. They are ideal for checking out new devices before they are installed in a model.

quite a few of the cheaper servos do not come with this information available.

What does it mean? The 20mm servo arm on (page 99) is a conventional item for a mini servo, with a rating of 20 grams per centimetre (20g/cm). This means that the maximum push/pull force would be at 1cm from the centre of the servo output shaft. This relates back to school physics, and the rules around the lever and fulcrum: doubling the lever length halves the force, while halving the lever length doubles the force. In this example, there would be 10g of force at the outer hole in the arm, but with twice the travel, and so on.

RECEIVER AERIALS

The wire aerial on the receiver is a tuned length, and the best range and least interference will be achieved if you leave it unbroken and at this original length. A 2.4GHz RX aerial is much shorter than AM or FM ones were, so you should not need to consider shortening them. It is not a good idea to think about lengthening them either.

To avoid water ingress, you can run the aerial wire up and out of the boat through a length of thin plastic tube with a cap on the end. This is not always necessary – quite often, simply laying the aerial horizontally will work. The range will probably be shortened a bit but, all things being equal, it should still be more than sufficient for normal boating operation. However, if the hull is moulded totally in carbon fibre, you will need to put as much of the aerial as you can outside, as signals are blocked by this material and the radio will not have any range at all.

DRY BATTERY RECHARGER

The dry battery recharger is a little device that can save you money in the long run. Many of the transmitters that RC boaters use are designed to work from 12 volts and to this end accommodate eight cells in the battery box. Eight dry cells x 1.5 volts = 12 volts, but if, like many people, you use eight NiMh cells, the voltage available is only 9.6 volts (8 x 1.2 volts). The only problem is that you have to throw the used dry cells away. Actually, despite what the manufacturers say, you can recharge certain dry cells, with some provisos. Do not use normal zinc chloride cells, especially cheap ones; they are very unlikely to recharge but will probably overheat! Always use alkaline cells. The trick is not to let them go totally flat before recharging. Once your TX shows signs of the voltage dropping, either on the meter or LED indicator, take out the batteries and recharge. Do not try to charge any type of dry cell with a normal LiPo charger.

There are several types of special charger available to buy. The Lloytron Smart Alkaline charger (model number B1551) will charge AA and AAA cells four at a time, individually, or a mixture of either. Although a previous model could also charge NiCad and NiMh cells, the current one will only recharge alkaline cells and nothing else. This model will not allow the accidental charging of the wrong type of cell. The charger display will show a faulty cell symbol and the device will fail to start charging. Good-quality alkaline batteries can be charged around six to ten times before they must be disposed of (safely).

There are a number of chargers for sale online that look identical to the Lloytron devices, but they are obviously copies and it might be risky to buy them. They are easily spotted as they do not have the Lloytron logo printed on the top of the case just above the LCD panel and are considerably cheaper. A £15 model from a reputable source is a better option – it will be worth it.

Lloytron Model B1551 dry-battery recharger. Alkaline cells can save money and give you more voltage for your TX than rechargeables, and this can increase the range of the system. Alkaline cells can be safely recharged around six times and sometimes a set can last a whole season.

The underside of the Lloytron charger, with the label that gives all the relevant information and proves that it is a genuine Lloytron item. To avoid buying a dud, look for this exact label.

The Lloytron charger will charge both AA and AAA cells together in any combination. A battery tester can also come in very handy. The advantage is that this tester adds a resistance to the cells to give a more realistic reading of the remaining capacity than just using a multimeter.

Chapter Eleven

Construction, Setting Up and More

BUILDING: KEEP IT LIGHT!

The combined weight of the motor, cell pack and radio gear is pretty much fixed, so weight savings can really only be made in the construction of the hull itself. Fast electric boats can be made from ABS plastic, glass-fibre-reinforced plastic (GRP), carbon-fibre-reinforced plastic (CFRP), wood or foam. Whatever you use, the key to a successful fast electric is to build it light. Light (within reason) equals fast; heavy (if overdone) equals slow.

If you are building a competition boat, remember that, while lightweight construction is desirable from the point of view of performance, the boat also needs to be strong enough to withstand the odd knock. Racing boats are not meant to touch each other during a race, but contact is often unavoidable, and no driver could truthfully claim never to have hit a course marker buoy!

If you are thinking of building a boat purely for straight-line speed record attempts, then you can afford to build it absolutely as light as is feasible, because it will not be running among other boats. You can use lighter components, which you might not want to use in a boat that needs to be capable of surviving a season's racing. One proviso is that you should not 'overdo the lightness' – at high speeds, any kind of crash could spell the end of the boat. There are places you can lighten, but you

The rudder servo on the cat. Note the helicopter-style ball-bearing pushrod connector.

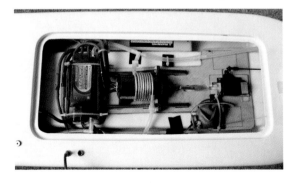

A nice neat installation in a cat. The steering servo had to be a mini one because there was not enough height in the boat for a standard unit, even on its side.

should make sure that any areas of stress in the hull are adequately reinforced.

The two main areas where strength is needed are around the motor mount and the transom of a surface-drive boat. The motor is the second-heaviest component after the cell pack, and the motor mount will be subject to quite a load when you bang open the throttle. GRP and epoxy-glass hulls can be quite thin and flexible in certain areas and may deform and pull out of shape under the weight and the torque of the motor. Use ply or FRP sheet doubler plates to spread the load across the hull, and strengthen the area where the batteries will sit.

The transom of a surface-drive boat has to carry the weight of the drive hardware and the load of the rudder when turning. With moulded FRP hulls, a simple doubling plate made from $^1/_{16}$ in ply is more than adequate to strengthen the transom. However, some hulls will already have been

reinforced in that area when the two halves of the hull were being joined. Hydroplanes need a good mounting for the turn fin as well as for the other areas, and servo arm and rudder arm connections also need to be secure.

The type of connector often used on the rudder arm of a cat or hydro. It is very easy to adjust, but it is often worth fitting an extra nut or some threadlock to lock it in place, as a single nut sometimes unscrews and drops off.

The completed cat. Sadly, it is no longer here, as this was the one that hit the concrete wall flat out!

The rudder servo in an outrigger hydro, using an aircraft-style adjustable clevis.

Another helicopter-type connector used on the rudder arm of my Mini Mono.

Hull Materials

The choice of material for the hull of a boat is influenced primarily by the cost and the volume of hulls being produced. The large manufacturers need high-volume, low-cost production and can take advantage of the economies of scale by producing thousands of a particular design. The individual builder also wants to keep costs as low as possible, but their priorities will be different from those of the big manufacturer. Often, they are looking for the best performance above all else and can take advantage of methods and materials that would be prohibitively costly for high-volume production. Each material has its own unique properties and problems, all of which need to be taken into consideration.

ABS Plastic

ABS plastic boats are usually made by vacuum-forming a pre-heated sheet of ABS over a metal pattern. The initial costs involved in tooling up to manufacture in ABS are quite high, but the process itself is fast and well suited to large volume production. Vac-formed ABS is the preferred method of hull construction for all the major manufacturers of kit boats. However, ABS has certain drawbacks as a material for making boats, apart from cost. Because the sheets of ABS are often formed over a male pattern, the important edges on the transom, spray rails, chine rails and other running surfaces are not as sharp as they perhaps should

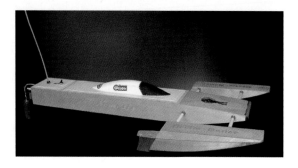

The last boat in my Electro-Marine Nemesis line. Built of wood, this model was actually my spare boat in the 12-cell class at the 1999 World Championships in the Czech Republic.

be. These edges will assume a radius, proportional to the thickness of the original sheet. Also, when asked to form over extreme changes in section, the sheet may thin excessively, and again chine and spray rails might not be as deep or pronounced as is desirable. These problems can be rectified using small amounts of car body filter to sharpen the radiused edges, but this is time-consuming and means the boat will need painting afterwards.

Well-made ABS-hulled boats can often be made to go as fast as FRP-hulled competition boats, but ABS is quite a dense material, so thin section sheet must be used to keep the weight down. It can also become rather brittle when cold and will tend to split or shatter in a crash. This is the reason why ABS-hulled boats are not raced alongside FRP-hulled boats.

ABS boats will usually be dimensionally accurate and nicely finished so do not always need to be painted, and ABS can be easily glued with super-glues. Epoxy glues such as Devcon and Araldite do not work on ABS, but there are several acrylic epoxy adhesives, such as Stabilit Express and Deluxe Materials Fusion, which bond well to ABS and give a much longer curing time to work with than the instant superglues.

FRP (Glass-Fibre- and Carbon-Fibre-Reinforced Plastics)

FRP is a catch-all term used to describe the various glass-reinforced plastics. These consist of a woven glass-fibre cloth or loose-strand matting laid up into a mould and impregnated with a polyester or epoxy plastic resin, which sets into a strong, rigid, lightweight material. Full-size race boat construction is very similar, often using lightweight closed cell foams sandwiched with carbon or Kevlar to produce an extremely strong and rigid hull capable of withstanding the punishment of racing offshore in high seas.

The FRP process involves making an original pattern, usually in two halves, over which FRP (glass cloth or strand mat, carbon, Kevlar or carbon/Kevlar cloth) is laid up to create a set of female moulds. These are then used to make production hulls. The surface finish of a hull made in this way will only ever be as good as the finish on the original pattern. Any defects on the pattern will be repeated on every production hull.

A release agent, typically a wax-based polish, is applied to the mould, then a gel coat, which can be coloured or pigmented, is painted or sprayed in. When this has gone off sufficiently, resin and cloth or matting are laid up to the required thickness, then allowed to cure, usually for twenty-four hours or more. The two halves are then joined together, with the two mould halves usually keyed with dowels to ensure accurate alignment.

Carbon fibre and Kevlar are very similar but are usually only used with epoxy resins and only come in woven cloth form. Carbon and Kevlar are much, much stronger than glass cloth, but are very much more expensive and difficult to work with. Although ultimately stronger, they are not as resistant to impact as epoxy-glass cloth and will tend to shatter or split, whereas epoxy glass will often deform and spring back.

The material cost of each individual FRP-hulled boat is higher than that of a boat with an ABS-moulded hull. The process of production is much more labour-intensive, slower and messier, with consistent results often dependent on the skill of the individual laminator.

The weight and strength of the finished product depends on how much resin and cloth or mat are used, and in this respect epoxy-glass cloth scores highly over polyester chopped-strand mat (CSM). A 1:1 ratio of resin to cloth gives the best strength to weight. Epoxy resin is stronger and more resilient than polyester resin and does not smell unpleasantly of styrene. CSM can absorb up to twice its own weight of resin, whereas cloth is more difficult to wet out and will absorb less. Polyester CSM is not as strong or resilient, tending to be rather brittle in comparison.

Wood

One of the best materials for making some types of boat is good old-fashioned wood. It is relatively cheap and easy to work with, light and strong, and

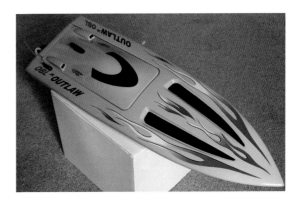

The OBL Outlaw, moulded from plastic.

with many differing grades and types, including balsa, ply and hardwoods such as oak and beech. Wood is a good material for making outrigger hydroplanes and catamarans, as the basic shapes are not very complex. Monohulls can be made quite well with wood, but they are more involved in some respects than outriggers and are harder to build straight. To be honest, it is easy to achieve the necessary sharp edges on the transom, chine and spray rails of monos, and on the ride areas of hydros and cats, but care must be taken when sanding down to a final finish to ensure that these do not become radiused or blunt.

Bare wood will soak up water and warp, so it needs to be sealed with epoxy or polyester resin, sanding sealer or dope. One or more coats of paint can then be applied over this. A polyurethane spray varnish can be flatted off for painting if required. Wood is surprisingly impact-resistant, is easy to glue with almost any adhesive, and can easily be repaired. To increase strength, different types of wood can be mixed together, for example, veneering balsa with 1/64in or 1/8in (0.4mm or 0.8mm) ply, or layers of very thin wing-skinning glass cloth can be applied when coating with resin.

Unlike the other methods of construction, working in wood does not require any sort of mould or pattern, as you are usually working from a plan or drawing. One of the great things about building in wood is that you are free to try out your own ideas. Also, the cost of building a wooden boat is only a few pounds or so, compared with approximately ten times as much for an ABS or GRP hull. The resulting look is rather different, of course – while some of the moulded hydro designs are very futuristic and eye-catching, a wooden boat can seem a little 'agricultural'.

One useful tip when you are using plywood in a build is to rub any area that you wish to glue with fine-grade sandpaper. Plywood is made by compressing the layers together between heated rollers. A release agent is used to stop the wood sticking to the rollers, and the residue of this can make sticking to ply difficult, especially when using superglues. Rubbing the area with sandpaper before glueing will remove the release agent and give sound joints.

Foam

White polystyrene foam and blue/pink styrofoam are very useful modelling materials that can be cut and shaped with a hot-wire cutter (there are videos online showing how to make your own cutter). Both types of foam can be sanded to shape and are very light. While not being particularly strong on their own, when veneered with balsa, ply or epoxy-glass cloth they form a very strong and light composite material, which is most often used for making outrigger-hydro and tunnel-hull sponsons.

To create anything from foam with a hot-wire cutter, you usually need to make up a set of pattern templates to cut around. To make holes in foam, another tip is to use a piece of brass tube sharpened at one end. Do not use a twist drill, as it will tear the foam and make an awful mess.

Foam can be glued with epoxy, PVA, or odourless cyano superglue. Avoid anything containing a solvent that could melt foam, such as conventional superglues and acrylic adhesives. Normal superglues will melt foam totally, leaving just a gooey sludge behind.

Gluing to GRP and Epoxy Glass

One of the biggest issues when building a boat with a GRP or epoxy hull is getting things such as motor mounts to adhere properly to the inside of the hull. It is not uncommon to see a GRP boat

after a minor crash with the motor mount having come loose. Despite a substantial fillet of epoxy glue, the mount has not been properly attached in the first place, and was just waiting for a hard knock to crack it off the bottom of the boat.

The simple reason for this is that GRP and epoxy resins excrete a wax-like substance as they cure. To get good, sound glue joints, it is vital to abrade the surface of the laminate with a coarse grade of wet and dry paper and then degrease the area with a solvent such as acetone or isopropanol.

Superglues can be used on GRP and epoxy glass, but the best adhesive is a two-part epoxy glue such as Devcon or Araldite. These can be thickened by adding micro-balloons (a very light, fine white powdery substance made from tiny hollow glass beads) when mixing the two parts of the glue. Micro-balloons make the epoxy stronger and easier to sand.

SETTING UP

Connectors

As connectors apply to ESCs, batteries and motors, they are included here under 'setting up'. An FE boat, especially a competition boat, will need quite a few connectors. The motor will need three bullet-type connectors, usually plugs, and the ESC will need three matching sockets to plug them into. At the other end of the ESC, you will need

My last pair of 3.5mm connectors (no longer used). They are Ideal for the smaller boat.

The Deans connector set is polarised, so it cannot be connected the wrong way. They are not up to handling today's power, but they are handy for some of the faster scale boats.

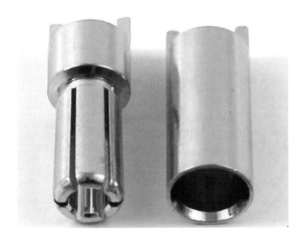

A full pack of 4mm plugs and sockets, used in the Mini classes.

EC5 connectors are popular in the USA but not much used in Europe. Like the Deans connectors, these are polarised, preventing incorrect connection.

A 5.5mm plug and socket, used in my 4S boats.

The XT60, another type of shielded and polarised connector. XT-style connectors are useful for conversion leads for chargers, and so on.

a connection to the battery. In the USA, there is a tendency to use the EC- and XT-type plugs and sockets. In the UK and Europe, there is a requirement to use safety loops on all MPBA- and NAVIGA-sanctioned competition boats, so separate bullet connectors must be used. The batteries have to be altered by removing the fitted plugs and soldering on a bullet plug on the negative lead and a corresponding socket on the positive lead. This then needs to be insulated with heatshrink tube.

Do not buy cheap connectors, especially from unknown vendors online. Get them instead from a reputable RC model store. Cheap connectors will probably have higher resistance, which means they could heat up and de-solder themselves. For four-cell boats, use 5.5mm bullet connectors and 4mm for anything smaller.

Cable

Good-quality cable is essential for top performance. Long lengths of thin cable will increase resistance and reduce the voltage available at the motor terminals and thus reduce power. Keep cell pack and speed controller leads as short as possible and use a decent brand of silicone-sheathed cable. This is especially important for brushless motors and controllers, where even a couple of inches of extra cable could potentially cause problems.

American cable sizes are often quoted in wire gauges. In Europe, cross-sectional area was used to differentiate between sizes, but now AWG

seems to be fairly universal. One question that newcomers on the FE forums often ask is what cable size to use. The answer is that it depends on how much current the cable will need to handle.

Below is a brief guide to using the three most popular gauges (the smaller the AWG number, the large the cable is):

14 AWG can handle around 65 amps continuous and around 105 amps for about 10 seconds or so before overheating.

12 AWG (most suitable for four-cell use) can handle up to 100 amps continuous and around 160 amps for around 10 seconds.

10 AWG is around 155 amps continuous and 250 amps for around 10 seconds.

These figures are not definitive, but they are a starting point. Also, it may not be advisable to allow a cable to get anywhere near the 70 degrees centigrade (around 150 degrees Fahrenheit) that these silicone-sheathed cables are supposed to be able to handle.

As well as motor and battery cables, this will have be factored in when making up safety loops for racing.

Good-quality wiring is needed to handle high currents. This is 12 AWG silicone-sheathed wire, used on my 4S boats.

A commercially made safety-loop set-up.

Safety loop on a Mini Mono.

Two recommended types of safety loop, which is a requirement of the NAVIGA racing rules.

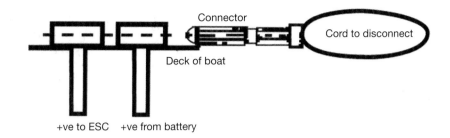

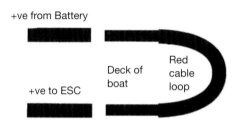

Soldering
Soft Soldering

Good-quality electrical solder joints are very important. Dry, crystalline joints will be weak and high in resistance. The key factors in achieving good solder joints are enough heat and clean oil- and grease-free conditions. A temperature that is too low will have you struggling to get any sort of joint, and the presence of oil and other contaminants will ruin any attempt at sound solder connections.

When you get it right, solder joints should be quick and easy. A bright and shiny appearance indicates a quality joint, while a dull, crystalline look indicates a poor-quality, dry joint, which will be prone to oxidisation and may fall apart. Dry joints can be caused by too little or too much heat, too little flux or bad-quality solder. The trick with soldering is to generously tin each half of the joint before trying to join it.

It is very handy to have a 12-volt DC-powered soldering iron for repairs at the lakeside. However, soldering outside can be difficult on a cold day, particularly if there is a breeze, as the iron will struggle to maintain temperature, especially if only rated at 25 watts or so.

Silver Soldering

Silver soldering is sometimes used to join the various parts of a stainless-steel hardware set and is also used to join flexible cable shafts to stub shaft ends. Silver soldering is very similar to soft soldering in principle, except that silver soldering is done at a very much higher temperature using a butane or propane-butane mix gas torch.

The solder itself comes in thin rods, with the flux in the form of a granular powder that is mixed with water to make a paste. The acids in the flux clean the joint and help the solder to flow. When the joint reaches red or orange heat, the solder can be applied by dipping it into the joint. Be careful, though, not to use too much solder. If the joint is a close fit and the flux is doing its job, the solder should flow under capillary action into the joint. After the joint has cooled, it needs to be cleaned. The flux can be very tenacious and can take a fair bit of effort to remove using a wire brush and wet and dry paper.

Although it is not essential to be able to silver solder, it is very useful to be able to carry out your own repairs, instead of paying someone else to do it for you.

BUOYANCY AND SELF-RIGHTING

A boat floats on the surface of the water because it is lighter than the water it displaces. If the boat fills with water, it will be no longer lighter than the water and it will sink. This simple principle cannot be emphasised often enough. Even experienced modellers often omit buoyancy material, trusting to chance that they will never need it. Instead, it is wise to assume that sooner or later the boat will end up full of water, for one reason or another.

Extra buoyancy can be added with scrap polystyrene foam and, if you put in enough, the boat should float even when it is completely waterlogged. Of course, this is not always possible, but it is worth trying.

IC boaters, who run boats with big holes in the top to help cool the engine, go to great lengths to add buoyancy. This is usually done by using two-part expanding foam, which is mixed together and poured into the front or sides of the hull. It is important to get the amount right, or the foam

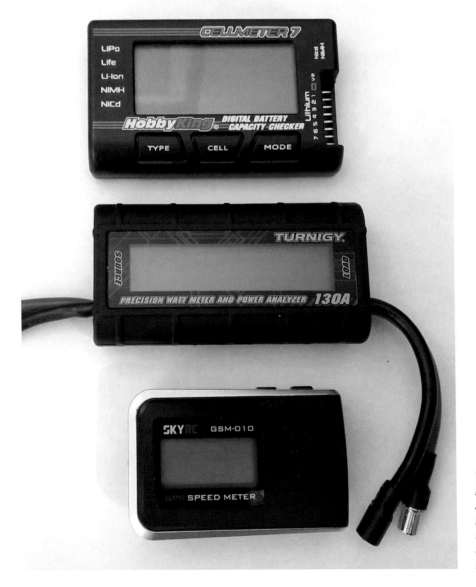

Three more useful items to have: another type of battery meter, a watt meter and power analyser, and a GPS speed meter.

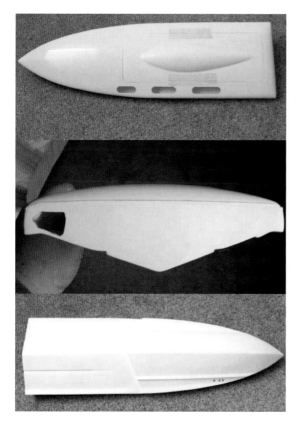

The anatomy of a flood chamber. When the boat is upside down, water floods in via the holes in the top of the boat and the large aperture at the rear, filling the flood chamber and causing the boat to turn back over. The chamber will empty again via the stern when the boat is moving forwards. The small holes in the bottom of the boat are vital as they let out the air in the chamber to allow the water in. Without them, the chamber may not fill and the boat will not self-right.

will expand and literally tear the boat apart, generating quite a bit of heat in the process. In any case, expanding foams are far too heavy for fast electrics. On these it is better to use scrap polystyrene blocks, packing beads or even cut-up swimming floats or 'noodles'.

Apart from in the USA, most modern surface-drive monohulls and all European Eco boats have some type of self-righting system. This allows boats that have flipped (or have been flipped) over and are left floating upside down to turn back over and continue running. Usually, a flood chamber is fitted on the left-hand side of the hull, but sealed on the inside. Several holes are made in the side of the hull to allow water into the chamber and air out. The largest hole is at the transom, which allows water back out of the chamber after the boat has righted itself.

With the boat upside down, the flood chamber starts to fill with water and as a result that side of the boat starts to sink. This has the effect of rotating the boat clockwise (viewed from the back) until it is right side up. Hitting the throttle will accelerate the boat and the water in the flood chamber will exit through the transom cut-out. It should be fairly obvious that, when water enters the flood chamber, air must be allowed to escape for it to fill fully. To facilitate this, small holes are usually drilled at the front end of the chamber in the hull bottom. When the boat is running, there is no water in the flood chamber, so performance is not affected. The self-righting action is helped by the fact that the battery is placed on the same side as the flood chamber.

PAINTING

Painting a boat is down to the owner's individual taste. All my boats are very simply painted, with visibility in mind rather than beauty. The first time someone goes over your work of art and leaves 'prop rash' on it, you will see why. The boats are fast and relatively small and you need to be able to identify yours clearly, so a bright, distinctive colour scheme is an important part of a fast electric racing boat. It is not unknown for competitors to lose sight of their boat in a flurry of spray and end up driving another boat with a similar colour scheme. It may sound unlikely, but it is true. A few years ago, somebody I know drove someone else's boat for an entire three-minute race, and only realised at the end when his boat was returned to him. It had been retrieved earlier from the reeds at the side of the lake. Similarly, if your boat flips over in a race – and it will at some point – the other drivers must be able to see it, so that they can drive around it, not over or through it. Because of these issues, NAVIGA and the MPBA have rules about colours for competition boats.

Fun-running boats may have as many coats of paint as you wish to apply, but the paint on a racing boat should be kept to the bare minimum. You can add a considerable amount of weight by spraying on fourteen coats of paint and three of lacquer! In addition, paint will build up on the sharp edges of the running surfaces on the bottom of the boat, blunting them and allowing water to creep up in the wrong places, causing drag or handling problems.

WATERTIGHT HATCHES

Some of the hatch systems dreamed up by the kit manufacturers are overly complicated (especially at the 'toy' end of the market), with sliding covers, gaskets and the rest. The more elaborate it is, the more likely it is to leak, especially after some usage. If you can tape down hatches carefully, you should not go far wrong. 'Hockey tape', which hockey players use around their socks and shin pads, is waterproof and adheres well to a hull.

If you have a moulded hatch made from ABS, GRP or epoxy glass, make sure you glue some buoyancy to it inside. If the hatch gets ripped completely off, it will probably sink, and getting a replacement may be difficult and expensive.

Rob Physick's L6 SAWs Outrigger Hydro battling some less than ideal water conditions for record breaking.

Chapter Twelve

H1 Outrigger Hydro Build

This chapter gives instructions for an easy way of constructing a three-point outrigger hydroplane. It is based on one of my designs for a traditional wooden 'rigger and incorporates a couple of updates from my original designs from the 1990s. The drawings for the boat were made in 2015. While it is not possible to include full-size drawings here, there are two full-page reproductions of the two sheet drawings. The text gives full instructions for building the boat but it can also be used as a generic guide to building wooden hydros. There are quite a few plans still available online. They may show a slightly different form of construction, but the methods can be adapted.

The design is for a European class Hydro 1 boat (2S to 3S). This is not a swish ultra-modern design, but a fusion of old and new, based on knowledge picked up during my time designing, manufacturing and running this type of boat. When I was manufacturing kits for hydros and cats, I had to come up with quick and simple ways of turning out the components, and the system of producing laminated balsa tub sides did speed up the process.

THE COMPONENTS
The Tub

The first part of the build is the body (commonly referred to as the 'tub'). Quite a number of the newer designs, especially those with moulded construction, have very slim, narrow tubs, and I initially considered this approach. However, apart from the fact that narrow tubs cause problems with fitting the internal equipment, the tub does have a part to play in the overall dynamics of a 'rigger. Although 'riggers rely on hydrodynamic lift from the sponsons, there is also an element of lift from the body (tub) of the boat. If you are running narrow sponsons, whilst there will be reduced drag there will also be less hydrodynamic lift, so the boat will rely more on the aerodynamic lift from the tub to keep it up. Clearly, a balance must be struck between aerodynamic and hydrodynamic lift. If there is too much aero, the 'rigger will blow off the water at every available opportunity. On this design, I decided to go with a wide-ish tub (although not as wide as my earlier designs) as I wanted to use narrow slab-sided (no anti-trip) sponsons.

The Sponsons

This was the first time I had designed sponsons without anti-trip and this narrow, so it was a bit of an experiment for me. Following on from the success of the JAE family of 'riggers, many boats are now appearing with the narrow sponsons without any anti-trip. However, not all of them work as well as the JAE boats. The idea of 'anti-trip' is to help prevent the outside sponson digging in during a turn and perhaps flipping the boat. The outside (left) sponson will try to dig into the water as the 'rigger tries to roll to the left in a right-hand turn. The angle on the outside of the sponson will allow an amount of slippage and lift to help keep the boat stable. That is the theory, anyway, but I have seen quite a number of boats without anti-trip that work all right without lifting the inside sponson too much. The turn fin on the right-hand sponson is there (in the first instance at least) to stop the boat from sliding too much and to keep it 'hooked up' in the turns. The sponsons are also placed further away from the tub than on earlier designs.

The Turn Fin and the Rudder

There is a close relationship between the rudder and turn fin. Without going into the technicalities too much, keeping the boat 'hooked up' in the turn simply means turning tightly and staying flat in the turn. It does not mean that you should automatically bend the turn fin into a curve. In fact, a straight, vertical turn fin creates less drag when running on the straight. If the boat is set up correctly, a vertical fin should keep the boat planted in the turns. It is also easier to keep the fin parallel with the tub; if it is not parallel, you will get drag. After all, you only want one rudder!

If a boat has been designed to work with a big curved fin, like the JAE boats, the chances are that it will not work correctly with a straight one. All my boats over the years have been designed to run with a vertical fin and they have been successful (especially the Nemesis) in several countries. In this design, now officially named Talisman after one of my earlier designs, I have again used the same basic turn fin as in all my others, but in this case I have lengthened it by 20mm to help prevent the outside (left) sponson digging in. You will also notice that the fin is angled backwards, there is a reason for this and it relates to the interplay between turn fin and rudder.

With a monohull, if you angle the rudder forwards slightly it will tend to lower the stern in a turn, thus lifting the bow and helping to prevent the bow dropping, and 'hooking' the boat. The same effect occurs in a 'rigger, although it may manifest slightly differently. Ideally, the inside sponson on a 'rigger should remain as flat as possible in a turn; angling the rudder slightly backwards

will lift the stern and keep the front end down and the same can be done with the turn fin. Angling the fin backwards (negative castor angle) can help keep the inside sponson planted in the turn.

Clearly, playing around with the relative angles of the turn fin and rudder can help a 'rigger to handle better. With a 'rigger, less is more and it may require just the odd millimetre of adjustment here and there. It is all part of the joy of setting up a 'rigger. They are probably the easiest of all boats to build, but they can be a pain to tune properly for maximum performance. I have not shown an adjustable turn fin on the plans for Talisman, but it would be easily arranged by putting a vertical slot in the rearward hole on the fin. The same could be done of course with the rudder if it does not come with adjustment capability.

The Booms

Some may not agree with my choice of material for the sponson booms, but it has worked for me for years: 8mm OD GRP kite tube and 11/32 K&S brass tube for mounting. This combination is better than thinner, lighter carbon tube, because the carbon tube is more likely to shatter if you hit a buoy at speed. The GRP tube is less brittle and exhibits a slight amount of flex under impact. This makes it easier to have a boat repaired and ready for the next heat.

The holes shown on the plan are sized to suit the 11/32 brass, but you can of course use thinner tube, as long as the hole centres remain the same.

MATERIAL AND TOOLS

The following tools are required to build per my plan:

- 9mm drill, 8mm drill and 2mm drill (plus other sizes to fit rudder pushrod, water-cooling tubes, and so on)
- Sharp craft knife
- Metal straight edge
- Dremel or mini drill with cut-off wheel to cut sponson tubes

- Mini plane and/or sanding blocks
- Hot-wire cutter to cut sponson cores

You will need the following materials to build per my plan (hurricanemodels.co.uk can supply almost all of the material needed):

- Card for templates (for example, heavy card stock from an artist's suppliers)
- Two sheets of 3/32 hard balsa (36in x 4in)
- One sheet of 1/64 (0.4mm) birch ply, at least 300mm x 800mm
- One sheet of 1/32 (0.8mm) birch ply, at least 300mm x 800mm
- Roll of double-sided carpet tape
- Blue or pink foam (large enough to cut two 360mm x 70mm x 40mm blocks
- Piece of 8mm dia. hardwood dowel
- Two 12in lengths of 11/32 OD K&S brass tube
- One 1-metre length of 8mm OD GRP kite tube
- Eight 2mm nuts and bolts
- 5-minute epoxy and/or medium odourless superglue (for foam) and accelerator.
- Material for jig (*see* building instructions)

BUILDING INSTRUCTIONS
Templates, Cutting Out and Laminating

First things first: you need some plans. Whichever plan you use, you will need to create cutting templates by transferring the image on to some medium (for example, heavy-duty card stock from an artist's supplier). Make sure the templates are exactly the right size. If you need to enlarge the plans, be aware that photocopiers enlarge by percentage area. For example, an A3 sheet of paper is double the size of an A4 sheet. If you have a printer, get two sheets of A4 paper out of the tray and place them side by side, long side to long side and that is the size of A3. However, if you put an A4 sheet on a photocopier and set it to magnify on to an A3 sheet, the drawing from A4 will not be the right size for your needs. If your

plans are not full size, take them to a print shop for accurate enlargement.

To help with this, mark a visual reference on each of the plan sheets. For example, draw a 300mm line on each sheet and check when the plans are printed that it measures the same. Obviously, the line may be thicker than as drawn (it may have a greater area) but the length will be correct.

Cutting out the balsa cores for the tub sides.

Using cyano to glue the balsa cores to 0.4mm ply.

The glueing pattern.

Whatever plan you have, once you have the templates cut out, mark the position of the bulkheads, the centres of the holes for the booms on the tub side template and the hole centres on the sponson template for the boom holes and the turn-fin mounts.

Using the tub template and a very sharp pencil, trace around the card shape on to the balsa. This will mark the balsa and leave a groove that a sharp knife blade will be able to follow when you come to carefully cutting out. Always use a really sharp knife when cutting balsa sheet. Even if the blade is only a little blunted, the balsa will have a tendency to tear across the grain, especially when the curves towards the front of the tub sides are being cut. Cut out two of the tub sides.

Take the sheet of 0.4mm ply and identify the slightly shiny, more 'finished'-looking 'outside' face. Glue the balsa pieces to the other (non-shiny) side of the ply and use a little weight on top to keep them flat. When dry, cut out the resulting assemblies from the ply sheet, using scissors or a sharp knife, then turn over the assemblies and glue the non-sheeted balsa side to the ply again and weigh it down to keep it flat. When this is dry, cut from the ply sheet and trim, to give two perfectly laminated tub sides with very little effort.

Medium cyano glue is best for attaching the balsa to the ply, as it dries quickly, with less likelihood of warping. Draw the outline of the tub side on to the ply, then apply the glue to the ply, not the balsa. There is no need to cover the area completely in glue. Just go around the outline with it, then go in a zigzag from one end of the shape to the other. If you clamp the pieces together before final shaping, you can make sure both sides are identical. Once the two sides have been lined up perfectly, use the template to mark the hole centres for the booms.

The bulkheads are laminated in the same way. Make sure they are all identical widths and square. The only difference is that the transom ('B5') is laminated with 0.8mm ply instead of 0.4mm like the others. You could make the others slightly thicker if you want.

Completing the Tub

The next step is to drill the tub sides for the booms, preferably on a pillar drill to ensure complete accuracy. If you are using the suggested booms (which is advisable), the holes should be drilled using a 9mm drill.

Completing the tub will be easier with a jig. This can be simply made by screwing two straight pieces of ½ to ¾in thick wood to a flat straight board. If you intend to make more 'riggers, you could use 1/16in by 1in aluminium angle with adjustment slots for different tub widths.

You will need to clamp the tub sides to help keep things aligned, as the quality and performance of the finished boat will depend on it having a straight, square tub. At least two small engineer's squares will be ideal for this purpose. Use greaseproof paper on the jig to prevent the wood sticking to it. Start from the transom (B5) and work forwards, making sure everything is square. When you get to the area where the booms go through the tub, the bulkheads (B2 and B1) should be tight up against the boom tube holes, but care should be taken not to block the holes in any way. Also make sure that the bottoms of the bulkheads are level with the bottoms of the tub sides.

Cyano may be used to glue everything, but you could also use 5-minute epoxy and have a little more time to work.

The final job before fitting the bottom skin is to glue a piece of 0.4mm ply across the back of the transom. This hides the ends of the tub sides

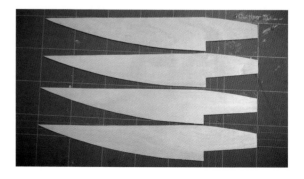

The four sponson sides cut from 0.8mm ply.

and generally neatens things up. Once glued and trimmed, the bottom skin can be fitted. There is no need for a template for this. Simply cut a piece of 0.8mm ply slightly longer and wider than the tub, lay it on a flat surface and glue the tub to it. Make sure that you do not introduce a twist at this point. You can use thick cyano and an accelerator for this job, but 5-minute epoxy will also work fine. Once it is set, trim it to suit.

You can fit a balsa nose block at this point, gluing and trimming to the curve of the nose. You may also want to strengthen the area on the tub floor where the motor is to be fitted. The tub can then be put aside, and all the brass boom sleeves can be prepared (see the measurements on the plan). Once they have been cut, now is the time to drill them if you intend to, using a 2mm drill and 2mm nuts and bolts. When they have been drilled, put the tubes to one side for fitting later.

Constructing the Sponson

Using the sponson template and a sharp pencil, carefully mark out four sponson sides on the 0.8mm ply. Cut them out with a sharp knife or scissors, then clamp then all together to make sure they are identical. Trim if necessary, but make sure you do not alter the planing angle or round off the point of the 'step'. You will need to drill two of the sides for the booms, using a 9mm drill if you are using the 11/32in brass tubes. The right-hand

The basic sponson shapes cut and sanded.

The holes in the sponson tops are filled with epoxy to secure the brass sponson tubes and the turn-fin mounts.

sponson side will need two additional holes drilled for the turn fin mounts. Use an 8mm drill here as the supports are 8mm hardwood dowel.

You will need a slice (or two) of blue or pink expanded foam or insulation board to make the balsa cores. The other dimensions are not vital, but the block of foam must be 40mm wide all the way through. To cut the foam, use two straight wooden battens drilled and pinned to the foam using 2in panel pins and a homemade hot-wire cutter. Make sure that the long edge of the block is perfectly straight and square; if not, sand it until it is. The top edges of the sponson sides go up against this edge and both sponson sides must line up perfectly.

Stick the ply to the foam with double-sided carpet tape, then use thin foam-safe cyano to seal all the edges. This should help to ensure that they never come apart! With slab-sided sponsons, stick one sponson side to the foam, aligning the top to the top edge of the foam, then use that as a reference to line up the other side. Using the sponson

Fixing the sides to the foam block using double-sided carpet tape works well. The actual sponson sides are used as the cutting templates.

sides as templates, cut out the shapes with the hot-wire cutter.

Use 0.8mm ply for the running surfaces and assemble in the following order. The little vertical piece at the 'step' is first. Cut slightly oversize, stick it to the foam with double-sided tape then seal the wood edges with thin foam-safe cyano. When set, trim to size. All the rest of the pieces follow the same procedure: cut oversize, stick with double-sided tape, seal edges with cyano, trim. Do the lower part of the sponson rear next and finally the rear of the sponson.

Next, sort out the actual running surface of the sponson, using the same construction method and 0.8mm ply. However, in this case, although

Completing the sponson sheeting using the double-sided carpet tape and super-glue method.

The bulkheads laminated in the same way as the tub sides ready to be squared up.

there is no overhang at the sides of the sponson, there is an overhang at the rear where the 'step' is. The overhang should be 2mm, but it is best left slightly longer and trimmed to the 2mm after everything is glued up. On this design, this 2mm overhang is very important for the correct running of the boat. Of course, this may not be the case with other designs. The top sheet is fitted in the same way. This is not done at this stage, although you can glue some balsa to the front of the sponsons to provide a nose block as with the tub. To cut the holes in the foam for the tubes, use a length of the brass tube as a tube cutter, gently pushing and rotating the tube to cut out a core so that the brass boom sleeves will fit perfectly. Make sure the holes go the full depth of the sponson. Cut the 8mm holes for the dowel turn-fin mounts in the same way (these may need to be done with an 8mm drill, which is not quite so neat, but it does work).

The final job is to make holes in the tops of the sponsons down into the holes for the boom tubes and fin supports. This is so that you can assemble everything and get it lined up perfectly and then dribble 5-minute epoxy into the holes, so that the tubes will be glued in without the need to disassemble anything.

Final Assembly

Measure and cut to length the two GRP booms (430mm each on this design) and fit the brass tubes into the holes in the tub. Measure the brass tubes on each side of the tub and centre them. Make some pencil marks on the tube outside of the tub so that you can quickly centre the tube later. Do the same for both tubes. Weight the tub so that it is flat on the bench and measure the ends of the tubes – both sides of the tubes should be the same distance from the bench. When you are happy with the height of the tubes above the bench, check to see that the tubes are square front to back with a try-square. When you have checked and double-checked that the boom tubes are straight and square, tack them in place with cyano to make sure they do not move. Mix some 5-minute epoxy and secure them well to the bulkheads and the tub sides, then go away and have a cup of tea!

The next job is to fit the turn-fin mounting dowels in the right-hand sponson. Cut two 40mm lengths and epoxy them into the holes. Leave them *slightly* protruding and sand flush with the sponson side when set. Drill pilot holes for whatever size screws you are going to use to secure the fin. This one was cut from 1/8in aluminium plate (although that could be thicker if you like) and drilled according to the plan. It is sharpened on the right-hand side only. It does not get fitted at this stage; this happens only after all the booms have been set up.

After spraying, the high-impact plastic (HIPS) decking is added.

Using a jig made from angle iron help keep the tub square during glueing – an earlier design being constructed.

The tub basically complete and awaiting sanding.

Test fitting before sealing the hull and spraying with polyurethane varnish.

Before you embark on the final assembly and set-up, clear your workspace so that you have a nice flat area. Insert the GRP booms through the brass tubes in the tub. Fit the brass tubes to the sponsons and slide the sponsons on to the booms. Chock up the rear of the tub so that it is parallel with the work surface and the sponsons sit square. With the sponsons parallel to the tub and each sponson spaced away from the tub as per the plan you have (130mm on this one), make sure the brass tubes are pushed fully into the sponsons. When everything is aligned, carefully mark on to the booms the positions of the brass tubes so that you can recentralise when necessary. Once you are happy with the set-up, do not touch it again. Just go and mix some 5-minute epoxy and dribble it in the holes in the top of the sponsons. Leave it for at least an hour, by which time everything should be nice and solid. At this point you could drill holes in the sponson tubes for securing bolts (2mm bolts here), once you have checked that the alignment is OK. You could also top the holes in the sponsons with more epoxy, but take care not to overfill.

Remove the sponsons and tubes. Use 0.4mm ply for the sponson tops and employ the same method as before: double-sided tape, sealing with cyano, trimming and lightly sanding to finish.

Before proceeding to the final steps, thoroughly waterproof the inside. Spray polyurethane varnish gives a nice hard glossy surface and can also be used for the finishing coat. Once the inside is dry, cut some foam to fill in between the two booms (*see* the cross-hatched area on the plan).

The decking can be one piece of 0.4mm ply from the nose to the transom, with the relevant cut-outs for access. Styrene sheet is a good material to use, as tape seems to stick to it better than to wood. Once it has been assembled and sanded, the boat is ready for grain filling, priming and painting – or you can leave the wood bare in all its glory. Screw on the turn fin, assemble the sponsons and booms, add the nuts and bolts (without over-tightening), and you are done!

You can use whatever drive system is recommended on the plan. Plans do not always specify

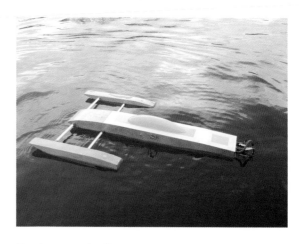

Ready to go, the first test.

The boat completed and ready to test.

The first test run of this design. It worked really well.

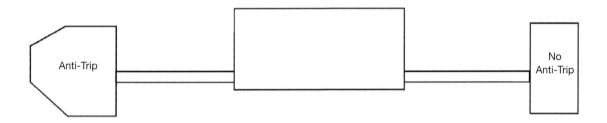

Sponsons with and without anti-trip.

a manufacturer, but you should definitely use a flexi drive. Fit the drive strut vertical and central on the transom, *not* offset. The motor can go anywhere in the compartment – there is usually plenty of space – as long as you bear in mind that you have to find room for an ESC and that the CofG should be somewhere around level with the turn fin. The steering servo RX, and so on, goes in the rear compartment.

The finished version of this boat works well. Although it is not used for racing, it is very enjoyable running it for fun.

The full plans of the 3-point outrigger hydroplane described in this chapter are available on request in PDF or DXF format by emailing hydroplans@outlook.com.

Liam Davison's HPR Cat 'Valkyrie' at speed. It has so far registered a GPS recorded speed of 108mph, but there is more to come.

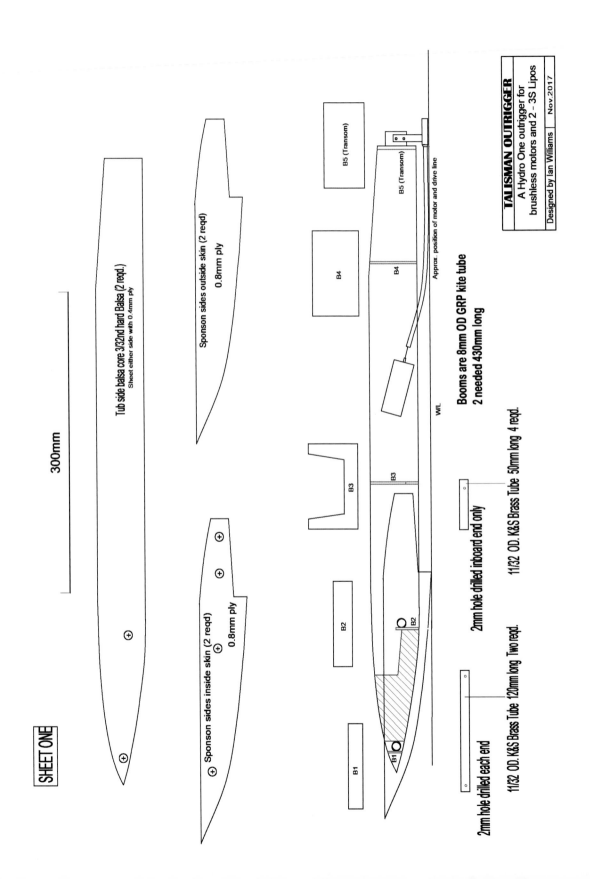

SHEET ONE

300mm

Tub side balsa core 3/32nd hard Balsa (2 reqd.)
Sheet either side with 0.4mm ply

Sponson sides outside skin (2 reqd)
0.8mm ply

Sponson sides inside skin (2 reqd)
0.8mm ply

B1

B2

B3

B4

B5 (Transom)

B5 (Transom)

wL

Approx. position of motor and drive line

Booms are 8mm OD GRP kite tube
2 needed 430mm long

2mm hole drilled inboard end only

11/32 OD. K&S Brass Tube 50mm long 4 reqd.

2mm hole drilled each end

11/32 OD. K&S Brass Tube 120mm long Two reqd.

TALISMAN OUTRIGGER

A Hydro One outrigger for
brushless motors and 2 – 3S Lipos

Designed by Ian Williams | Nov.2017

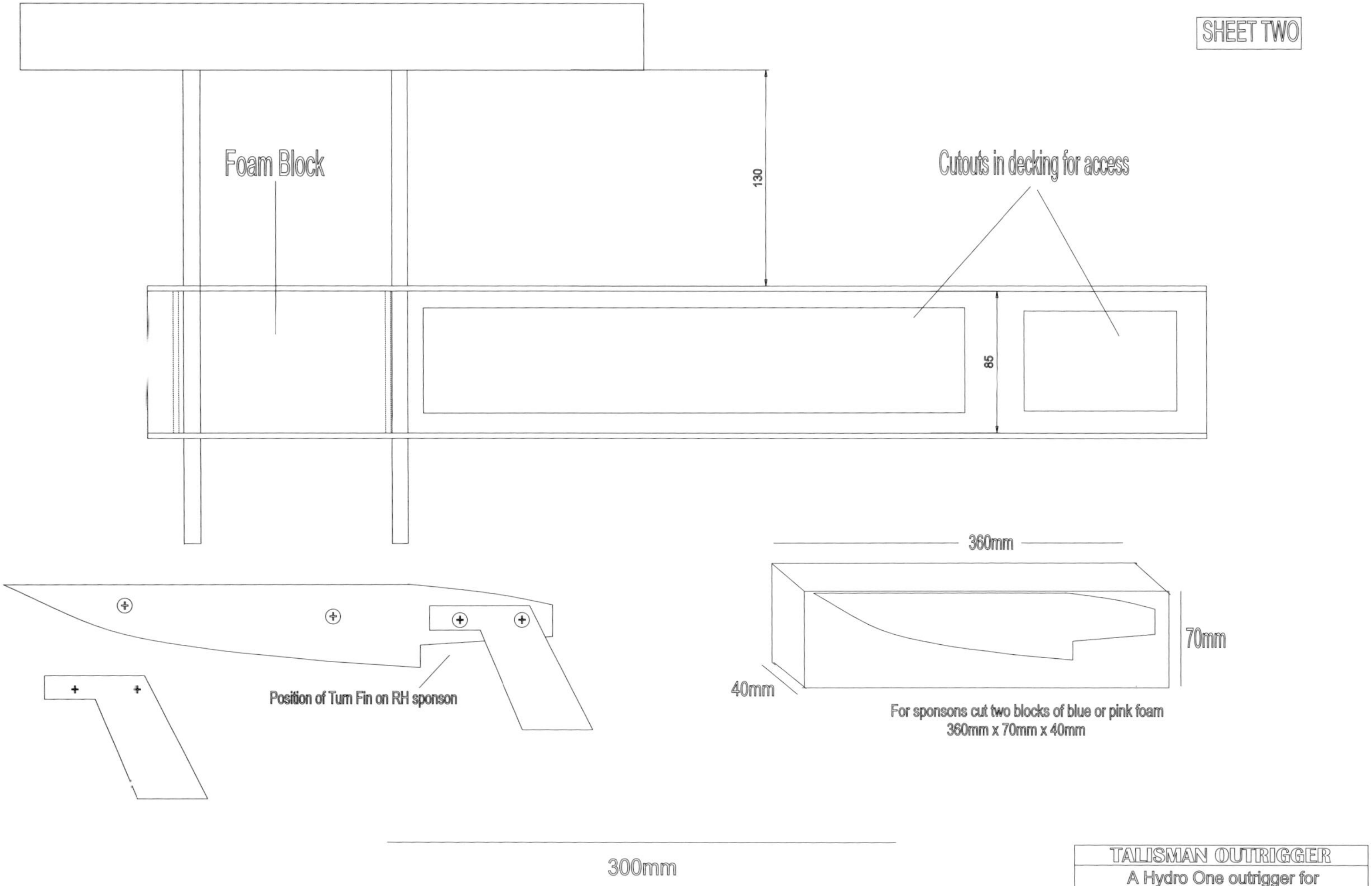

SHEET TWO

Cutouts in decking for access

85

130

Foam Block

70mm

360mm

40mm

For sponsons cut two blocks of blue or pink foam
360mm x 70mm x 40mm

300mm

Position of Turn Fin on RH sponson

TALISMAN OUTRIGGER	
A Hydro One outrigger for brushless motors and 2 - 3S Lipos	
Designed by Ian Williams	Nov.2015

Chapter Thirteen

Racing and Straight-Line Speed Records (SAWS)

Some boaters are happy to speed around a lake with a fast boat they have just built or purchased, but if you get bored boating on your own, you might really enjoy racing against other like-minded owners. If you have not raced before and want to have a go, the first thing to do is to contact either a local club or the MPBA Fast Electric Section, who will be able to put you in touch with the right person or place. Whether you want to race at club or national level, you will need to ensure that any boat you build or acquire conforms to the relevant rules and regulations for the class that interests you. Many clubs in the UK base their competition rules wholly or partly on the MPBA-FES regulations, making it easy to run at both local and national level. Although reading a copy of the rules will hopefully give you some useful ideas and information, when building your first fast electric it will be very useful to have an experienced modeller on call to help you out with the construction and the correct trimming afterwards.

If you are in the UK and running a fast boat anywhere, whether in competition or not, you would be well advised to join the MPBA, if only for the high level of third-party liability insurance it provides.

RACING CLASSES AND COURSES

The MPBA-FES mainly runs the classes that are raced under the NAVIGA banner. There are some differences between these and the MPBA classes,

especially regarding batteries and limiters, so the latter are covered later.

FE racing is controlled by the M section of NAVIGA. There is one IC class also included. The basics are covered here, but if you want more information on all the class rules and technical details, have a look at the NAVIGA website (naviga.org) and click on the 'Section M' tab at the top of the page.

At most race meetings, including the National Championships, there will be at least three heats

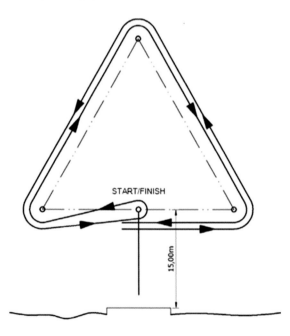

NAVIGA triangle course, used for F1E and the Eco classes. (Diagram extracted from NAVIGA website with permission of the President, Walter Geens)

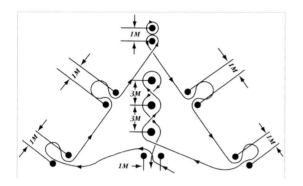

The Christmas tree triangle course for F3E steering.

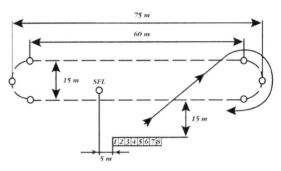

Standard NAVIGA and MPBA oval for all surface-drive classes.

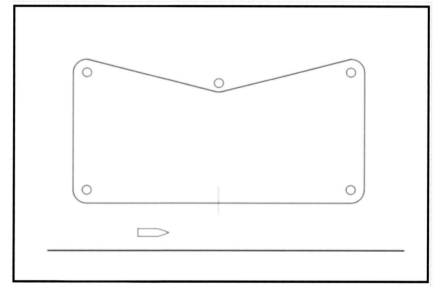

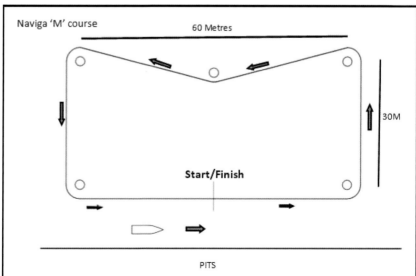

The NAVIGA M course, used for FSRE and sometimes in the UK for Eco classes.

of each class. The final positions are determined from a participant's two best race scores, so it is possible to have one bad race and still do OK. Most competitors race in two classes. Some may take part in three or more, but keeping more than two boats fully prepared during the day can be a challenge.

NAVIGA Classes

F1 – Solo race, triangle course

F1-E – model boats with electric motor (No Motor Limit), no overall weight limit, battery voltage limited to 43V with a maximum battery weight of 1400g LiPo.

F1-V – IC-powered boats limited to 3.5, 7.5 or 15cc.

The idea is to go around the NAVIGA triangle in both directions against the clock (with a hairpin turn on the bottom straight) in the fastest time.

F3 – Solo race, steering, triangle course (Christmas tree)

F3-E – model boats with electric motor (no motor limit), battery voltage limited to 43V and a maximum battery weight of 1400g LiPo.

F3-V – model boats with combustion motor.

Run around a triangular (NAVIGA triangle based) track in a set order against the clock. Points are deducted for every missed or touched buoy.

Eco – Submerged-drive, multi-race, triangle course

Eco Mini Expert – Electric-powered model boats (no motor limit), minimum model weight 450g, max. length 430mm (without start number plate), max. battery weight 110g.

Mini Eco Team – team race (a minimum of 2, max. 3 racers, max. 3 models per team). Race time is 18 minutes (3 x 6 minutes).

Eco Expert – Electric-powered model boats (no motor limit), minimum model weight 1kg, maximum battery weight 280g.

Eco Team – team race (min. 2, max. 3 racers, max. 3 models per team).

Two teams of 3 competitors (3 competitors race in a group for 6 minutes respectively (18 min for teams) around the NAVIGA triangle, anti-clockwise. It is permissible to circle around a missed buoy.

Mono – single-hull model boat, multi-race, surface-drive, oval course

Mini Mono – single-hull, electric motor (no motor limit), min. model weight 450g, max. hull length 450mm, 6-minute race, max. battery weight 113g.

Mono 1 – single-hull model boat with motor, 6 min race, max. battery weight 280g.

Mono 2 – single-hull model boat with electro motor, 6-min race, max. battery weight 560g.

Up to 6 competitors race in group for 6 minutes around the NAVIGA oval, clockwise. Circling around missed buoys is not allowed, penalties are given for every missed buoy.

Hydro – multi-hull model boat, group race, oval course

Mini Hydro – multi-hull model boat with electric motor (no limit), min. model weight 450g, max. length 450mm, 6-min race.

Hydro 1 – multi-hull model boat with unrestricted electric motor, 6-min race.

Hydro 2 – multi-hull model boat with unrestricted electric motor, 6-min race.

Six competitors race in a group for 6 minutes around the NAVIGA oval, clockwise. Circling around missed buoys is not allowed, penalties are given for every missed buoy.

FSR – group race, M course

FSR E – single-hull model boat with unrestricted electric motor, 15-min race, battery voltage limited to 43V, max. battery weight 840g in LiPo (battery changes are not allowed).

A maximum of 8 competitors race in group around an M course anti-clockwise. Circling around missed buoys is allowed.

All multi-racing classes must use limiters except the Mini Mono and Hydro classes (although this may change one day). Up-to-date information is available on the NAVIFGA website.

UK Classes

The UK classes are the same as the NAVIGA ones, with some minor differences. At national level, surface-drive classes are the main focus. F3E and F1E are not run and the two Eco classes are run only if there is enough interest that year.

The rules on batteries and on the use of limiters are more relaxed in the UK in comparison with the NAVIGA ones (*see* mpba-fes.org.uk; click on the 'Racing' tab and follow the link just under the photos of the classes that appear).

USA Racing

Again, there are a number of differences between European, UK and US racing. For example, most oval racing is over a set number of laps rather than a fixed duration, and there are none of the submerged-drive classes that are run in Europe. The North American Model Boat Association (NAMBA) does not allow stepped hulls in the mono classes, except for the offshore class. However, as this is a scale class, self-righting is not allowed. The International Model Power Boat Association (IMPB) has also banned stepped hulls.

For more detailed information on all the classes, have a look at the websites of the two main RC boat organisations in the USA: namba.com and impba.com.

GENERAL POINTS ON RACING

Multi Racing

'Multi racing' is so called because it involves the racing of multiple boats around a course simultaneously, instead of single boats racing against the clock. In the early days, the radio equipment did not allow the running of more than one boat at a time, and there are still classes such as Steering and FIE Speed that have boaters competing alone against the clock. Although there are no regulations in the F1 and F3 racing classes limiting hull form or the type of drive system, a submerged-drive monohull will be a better choice than a surface-drive boat for negotiating the triangular anti-clockwise course. This is because this type of course demands precise handling and the need to turn tightly in both directions, which more or less precludes the use of surface drive. Because most monohulls are self-righting, they also make excellent fun-running boats, as they can be run in ridiculously rough conditions. When they fall over, they just roll upright again!

Oval Racing

The format for oval racing is slightly different. The boats are all surface-drive models and race clockwise, turning right only. Surface drive gives

The drivers' rostrum at the Bridlington MBS club, with the race control cabin underneath. This is possibly the only one of its kind in the UK.

superior straight-line speed over submerged drive, but with a trade-off in acceleration and handling. The boats start from rest and go to the top right buoy and clockwise to the start line halfway along the main straight.

It is not enough to have a really fast boat if you cannot drive reasonably neatly, avoiding the turn marker buoys and the other boats. Any sort of contact with a solid object can cause damage to your boat and put you out of a race. Catamarans and hydroplanes run the risk of trapping a marker buoy between the front sponsons, and monohulls with sharp bows can embed themselves in the soft foam from which the buoys are often made. Both of these incidents would lead to an early withdrawal from the race, so it pays to give yourself plenty of room.

The best racing boat is one that is easy to drive, leaving the owner free to concentrate on what is happening around them. If the handling is twitchy and nervous, the boat will be a handful to drive, even when simply blasting up and down an empty lake on its own. Trying to control it around a tight oval course among a pack of other boats could prove to be quite problematic. Most people will forgive the odd incident, but if you make a habit of crashing into others, you will not be popular. The basic advice is to keep your head, drive a neat and tidy course, and try to stay out of trouble. Common sense is the most valuable tactic when racing.

Racing Etiquette

If you are running on the recognised racing line, the onus is on the other drivers to find a way past if they want to overtake. Experienced drivers will make allowances for those who are less experienced, so a novice should stick to their line and not weave around in an attempt to make it easier for others to overtake. In fact, it will just make it harder if you make unexpected manoeuvres.

If you have to come into the pits for some reason – for instance, if you get something wrapped around the prop – take care when re-joining the race. Do not simply drive straight out into the path of the other boats. They will be travelling at full

A collection of Club 500 boats. This restricted one-design class is not really all that fast but it is enjoyable and quite popular with scale clubs.

A collection of models set up ready for a speed event: (left to right) L3 Hydro, L3 Mini Hydro, L3 Mini Mono. L2 Mini Cat and L2 Mini Mono.

My L3 surface-drive mono moving at speed.

A good-looking Chinese RTR boat available online. It seems to have the right design features for racing, so might be worth checking out.

Left to right: L3 Mini Mono, L3 Mono and L6 Mono.

speed; you will not. Take a wide line into the first turn until it is safe for you to pick up the racing line again. If you drive inside a turn marker buoy, you will incur a 5-second time penalty; you are not allowed to circle the buoy, as in the past. You will probably have other boats bearing down on you at speed, so it is not a good idea anyway. If you miss more than a few marker buoys, you start to lose laps, so drive neatly.

The main thing to remember above all else is that everyone races model boats for fun, not to prove a point, or for any other reason. Always have some consideration for other boats and their owners.

Racing adds a fascinating element to the hobby of fast electric model boats. It is so much more than simply blasting around the local pond upsetting the owners of the scale boats. Most fast electric meetings are very relaxed and friendly,

My Hydro & Marine Intruder cat is a good fast oval-racing boat on 4S.

This Chinese RTR boat has had good reviews, but it is non-stepped, so may not fare very well against stepped boats.

Slightly blurred photo of a boat doing around 80mph.

and participants tend not to take themselves too seriously.

STRAIGHT-LINE SPEED RECORDS (SAWS)

The setting of speed records holds a fascination for some people. The idea of building a boat that is as lightweight as possible and with the greatest amount of power is certainly a challenge, and pure speed machines can be very exciting to drive. In the UK and the USA, the speed course is a straight line between two buoys 110 yards apart (1/16 mile). The course is run once each way and the speed registered is the average of the two times. In Europe, the course is 100 metres in length and the speed is quoted in kilometres per hour rather than miles per hour.

As there are a number of classes available, it is worth searching online for the websites of the relevant organisations, which give full information on current records and classes.

The Wilkinson Sword Trophy (a real sword) is presented to the competitor with the fastest speed of the day at the UK SAWS.

Arne Hold's 187mph L6 Hydro. The speed record was set at the Munich SAWS.

UK SAWS Records as of 2021

Hull Type/Class	Date	Venue	Entrant	Speed (mph)
Hydro (Mini) L02	12/9/21	Carr Mill Dam	David Harvey	38.79
Hydro (Mini) L03	12/3/17	Dearnford Lake	David Harvey	46.973
Hydro (Scale) L02	12/3/17	Dearnford Lake	David Harvey	28.662
Hydro (Scale) L02 (brushed)	15/9/02	Warminster	Allan Shillitto	33.88
Hydro (Scale) L03	26/10/14	Dearnford Lake	David Harvey	40.19
Hydro (Scale) L04	08/9/07	Branston Water	Peter Barrow	56.39
Hydro (Scale) L06	31/10/10	Watermead	Peter Barrow	51.07
Hydro (Scale) L08	12/9/21	Carr Mill Dam	Rob Scott	44.56
Hydro (Scale) L09, L10, L20 L Open.	No Record			
Hydro L01	No Record			
Hydro L02	26/4/15	Dearnford Lake	David Harvey	39.181
Hydro L02 (brushed)	15/9/02	Warminster	Bill Hickman	32.75
Hydro L03	12/3/17	Dearnford Lake	David Harvey	51.165
Hydro L04	28/10/12	Branston Water	Paul Upton Taylor	56.63
Hydro L04 (brushed)	15/9/02	Warminster	Chris Osman	44.73
Hydro L06	24/4/16	Dearnford Lake	Paul Upton Taylor	84.26
Hydro L06 (brushed)	15/9/02	Warminster	Chris Osman	44.16
Hydro L08 and L09	No Record			
Hydro L10	15/9/02	Warminster	Carl Dawson	51.05
Hydro L20 and L Open	No Record			
Mono (Mini - SubSurface) L01	14/7/19	Larkfield Dam	Nigel Turner	14.25
Mono (Mini - SubSurface) L02	31/10/10	Watermead	Mark Shipman	29.54
Mono (Mini - SubSurface) L03	26/10/14	Dearnford Lake	Mark Shipman	22.72
Mono (Mini - Surface) L02	12/3/17	Dearnford Lake	John Croyden	39.353
Mono (Mini - Surface) L02 (brushed)	30/7/05	Herrington	Joe Read	30.12
Mono (Mini - Surface) L03	28/10/12	Branston Water	Rob Physick	33.55
Mono (Scale) L02	No Record			
Mono (Scale) L03	No Record			
Mono (Scale) L04	14/7/19	Larkfield Dam	Rob Physick	43.56
Mono (Scale) L06	29/4/18	Larkfield Dam	Rob Physick	48.21
Mono (Scale) L08	12/9/21	Carr Mill Dam	Rob Physick	45.16
Mono (Scale) L09, L10, L20 and L open	No Record			
Mono (SubSurface) L01	12/9/21	Carr Mill Dam	Nigel Turner	15.29
Mono (SubSurface) L01	29/4/18	Larkfield Dam	James Hobbs (Junior)	15.18
Mono (SubSurface) L02	31/10/10	Watermead	Mark Shipman	30.37
Mono (SubSurface) L03	26/10/14	Dearnford Lake	Donatas Ceponis	31.84
Mono (SubSurface) L04	08/9/07	Branston Water	David Harvey	32.2
Mono (SubSurface) L04 (brushed)	30/7/05	Herrington	Joe Read	28.23
Mono (SubSurface) L06	26/10/14	Dearnford Lake	Mark Shipman	24.94
Mono (SubSurface) L08, L09, L10, L20 and L open	No Record			
Mono (Surface) L01	29/4/18	Larkfield Dam	Christopher Hobbs	21.47
Mono (Surface) L02	26/4/15	Dearnford Lake	Rob Physick	45.248
Mono (Surface) L02 (brushed)	15/9/02	Warminster	Bob Walden	32.58
Mono (Surface) L03	27/10/13	Dearnford Lake	Rob Physick	49.07
Mono (Surface) L04	12/3/17	Dearnford Lake	Rob Physick	54.745
Mono (Surface) L04 (brushed)	20/9/03	Herrington	Ken Brown	34.72
Mono (Surface) L06	29/4/18	Larkfield Dam	Keith Mallam	58.06
Mono (Surface) L06 (brushed)	17/10/04	Herrington	Ian Philips	35.8
Mono (Surface) L08	28/10/12	Branston Water	David Harvey	45.82
Mono (Surface) L09	No Record			
Mono (Surface) L10	20/9/03	Herrington	E Lazenby	36.53
Mono (Surface) L20	No Record			
Mono (Surface) L Open	No Record			
Tunnel (Mini) L02	31/10/10	Watermead	Martin Cusick	28.01
Tunnel (Mini) L03	12/3/17	Dearnford Lake	Rob Physick	30.222
Tunnel L01	No Record			
Tunnel L02	24/4/16	Dearnford Lake	Rob Physick	34.49
Tunnel L03	27/10/13	Dearnford Lake	Rob Physick	39.82
Tunnel L04	24/4/16	Dearnford Lake	Ian Williams	47.94
Tunnel L06	12/3/17	Dearnford Lake	Keith Mallam	53.957
Tunnel L08	14/7/19	Larkfield Dam	Keith Mallam	55.57
Tunnel L08	28/10/12	Branston Water	Rob Physick	41.28
Tunnel L08	31/10/10	Watermead	Brian Barrow	30.66
Tunnel L09	No Record			
Tunnel L10	14/7/19	Larkfield Dam	Keith Mallam	46.46
Tunnel L20	12/9/21	Carr Mill Dam	Keith Mallam	86.62

Chapter Fourteen

FE Power in Scale Boats

It can be difficult to get a kit-built scale model of, say, a vintage hydroplane to work well. Often, the reason why an owner will struggle to get such a boat on the plane is because it has been built exactly to plan. This may seem counter-intuitive – surely, building it according to the instructions is a good thing – but scale boats can turn out to

Rich Marsh's K41 scale hydro Miss Windermere 4, *which was powered by a Jaguar engine. The model is brushless-powered.*

K41 at speed.

be quite heavy due to the materials used in the kit construction. The motor and battery set-up advised in the instructions may not be appropriate either. Sometimes, the motor will be a standard brushed type with not much power, and NiMh cells only increase the overall weight.

It would be wrong to downplay any type of model boat – scale models of tugs, lifeboats and warships all have their place – but it is certainly worth looking at subjects that most scale modellers would not consider. These might include scale models of historic speed-record breakers such as Donald Campbell's *Bluebird* and Ken Warby's *Spirit of Australia*.

While some FE racers build scale boats of varying types, it seems that few dedicated scale modellers would even think about building a fast electric boat, except perhaps for the odd MTB, police boat, lifeboat, and so on. The aim here – with a foot in both camps, so to speak – is to encourage you to think about building a fast electric scale model, and to explain some of the differences in construction technique between the two types. This is not about building an all-out competition boat, but a boat that will perform in a scale-like manner, like any other scale model you might build, only a bit faster!

BUILDING LIGHTNESS IN

Remember, it is easier to add weight to a boat than it is to remove it. With that in mind, you

The Aeronaut Spitfire. This very nice wooden kit is still available from Hobbies (hobbies.co.uk).

The Spitfire runs very well on the vintage-looking outboard. It uses an outrunner brushless motor.

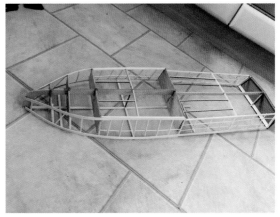

'Building in lightness': Rich Marsh's Miss England 3 *framed up.*

Miss England 3 *with the other two* Miss England *boats.*

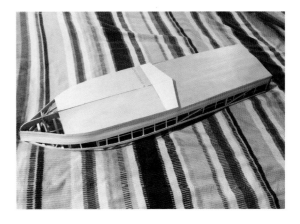

Starting to sheet the underside and construct the step.

need to look at the slightly different construction techniques. More often than not, a scale model owner does not have to worry too much about the weight of their boat. Obviously, it depends on the type of model, but they are more likely to have to *add* weight to bring the hull down to its designed waterline. This is the opposite of what you want with a fast electric racing boat, where the hull needs to be light to offset the weight of the batteries and relatively large motors. The same applies to models of records boats and other fast craft, which often do not have a visible waterline!

Clearly, it is better to build lightness in than to try to lighten a heavy boat retrospectively. How you do this will depend on the type of model you are building and whether it is a kit or a scratch-build from plans. If it is a kit, what is the method of construction? Is it all wood built up construction, possibly plank on frame or with a GRP-moulded hull that has wooden frames and bracing and perhaps a wooden deck? Whatever the type of construction there are ways to build as light and strong a model as possible.

There are several ways of building in lightness, but there is one major method for saving weight, which will be relevant in a couple of scenarios. Plans for scratch building will usually give suggestions for materials to be used, and builders generally tend to follow that advice. Almost certainly, plywood will feature somewhere and this will usually be the case for any kit-built boats featuring all-wood construction. Alternatively, a kit may include a GRP hull along with ply components for bulkheads, various support structures

A fantastic model of Dixie 2. *This was the last displacement hull to hold the speed record. (Courtesy of Rich Marsh)*

A nice model of Miss London.

Miss England 1. *The original was built for Henry Seagrave in 1929 by the British Power Boat Company. It was designed by Hubert Scott-Paine, who was the brains behind many fast torpedo and gun boats during World War II.*

and so on. If you replace the ply parts with parts made using the balsa and ply laminate method (*see* Chapter 12), you could achieve a weight reduction of between 5 percent and 20 percent compared with the original build spec.

The method is described in the instructions for building a hydroplane (*see* Chapter 12), but it is worth recapping and expanding on it. The laminate is made from balsa and the thinnest 3-ply marine, which is 0.4mm (about 1/64in) thick. This is very easy to work as it can be cut with scissors. The hard balsa core is usually 1/8 or 3/16in and the ply is glued on either side using medium or thin cyano. The balsa thickness can vary, but the thin ply should still be used. This type of laminate provides a very light but very strong material, especially if you can arrange to have the grain of the ply and balsa run at 90 degrees to each other. Most of the pieces where ply is used in the model – frames, deck supports, whatever – can be swapped out for pieces made from this laminate. The trick is to cut the shapes required out of the balsa core first, then glue them to the sheet of ply. When the pieces are dry, cut them very carefully from the ply using the core as a template. The lamination can then be completed by glueing the other side of the shape (frame, bulkhead, and so on) on to the ply sheet. If you are making frames and ribs, leave cutting out the centres until the glue is fully dried, then trim to the exact shape required.

One little tip when using this method is to seal and harden the edges of the laminate (especially for ribs, frames or bulkheads and so on) with thin cyano. Use surgical gloves, or a sandwich bag to

Rich Marsh's Miss Super 3 *scale hydro. (Courtesy of Rich Marsh)*

A fantastic model of Don Gar's Miss America X.

Miss England 2, *another beautiful model owned by Rich Marsh.*

protect your fingers, smear the cyano all around the edges and leave to dry.

The result of using this method is a material that is lighter and more stable than plywood and easier to seal. If you replace all the ply components with it, or at least as many of them as is feasible, you will save a significant amount of weight.

Further actions you can take to keep the weight down during construction include using styrene sheet instead of wood (if feasible) for any cockpit, hatch or superstructure detail. Weight savings can also be made in the motor/drive/hardware area.

GOING BRUSHLESS

If you are building from a kit or a plan, it may well specify a brushed motor (often a 540 type). You do not have to go brushless in order to have a quick scale boat, but brushless motors do have a better power to weight ratio than brushed motors. (Also, by the way, brushless motors and ESCs do not have to use LiPo batteries. They can use NiMh or NiCad batteries. Likewise, brushed motors and ESCs can get their power from LiPos!)

It is a fact that a brushless motor will be more powerful than a brushed motor of the same size. There are many technical reasons for this, but basically the extra power provides a few more options when choosing a motor for a specific boat. If you are building from a kit or plans that specify a standard 540 brushed motor, you could use a smaller brushless motor of equivalent power, especially if you wanted more internal room or are looking to save weight. Alternatively, you could use a roughly 540-sized brushless motor to give you a lot more power.

Brushed 540 motor specs are a bit of a mine-field and quite difficult to work out. The most common 540 motor is the Mabuchi (or derivative) RS540SH-7520. This has a maximum stated voltage of 7.2 volts, although it can take higher voltages if it is not overloaded. The physical size is 35mm can diameter and 50mm can length.

That equates physically to a 3550 inrunner brushless motor. The RS540SH-7520 specs state that maximum revs at 7.2 volts are 23,400, while maximum efficiency is at 19,750rpm. Dividing the maximum rpm by the voltage will give a figure that is roughly equivalent to the Kv rating of a brushless. In this case, 23,400 divided by 7.2 = 3250Kv. As there are other factors involved, this is a huge simplification and should be taken as a guide only, but it does give an idea of the type of brushless motor you will need.

If you use a two-cell (2S) LiPo pack and choose a brushless motor of around 3000Kv, the set-up will have much more power than before. Brushless motors have a lot more torque than brushed 540s and will stand higher loads before effective rpms drop. Another advantage is that they do not have brushes that wear out! Although brushed motors are quite a bit cheaper than brushless, given the same operating conditions, a brushless one will last a lot longer. I have one 3660 sized brushless motor I regularly raced with (a Hacker B50 11 L) that is over twelve years old. It is not used for racing now, as racing has progressed and higher Kvs are needed, but it is still in good working condition and is now used for initial trials of new boats.

Another notable factor is that, unlike most brushed motors, brushless types do not have a preferred direction of rotation. This is helpful when you are using two motors and want them to rotate in opposite directions.

Plastic kit model of an MTB, motorised with two small brushless motors and ESCs, with mixing done from the transmitter.

If you want to go with the smaller lighter motor, it stands to reason that something like a 2860 (can diameter and length) with a Kv of around 34 to 3600Kv would work well. However, this type of motor will not display as much torque as the larger 3550 motor, which will probably mean you will have to run with a smaller-diameter prop. Another option would be to use an outrunner brushless of around the same Kv. An outrunner is more 'torquey' than an inrunner.

Most of the time, as with almost all other scale boats, the type and purpose of the hull will determine the motor type. For example, you would probably choose a powerful torquey motor for a scale tug. In addition, the aim with scale boats is to run them in a lifelike manner and at a scale speed that looks right. As an example, I have a 30in model of an offshore catamaran that has run with an uprated motor at around 50mph on 4S LiPos. If that was an exact scale model based on the same hull, a speed of 20 to 25mph would be more than adequate. Mine gets fully on the plane at around 15mph and looks fine – if you are not used to running any kind of fast boat, 15mph is quite quick enough!

RUNNING GEAR

This is a tricky subject for models of fast scale boats, especially of record-breaking craft, as you may have to deviate from scale appearance. Builders of model tall ships sometimes have to fit an extended keel and rudder to make the boat sail correctly. It may not look great on dry land, but in the water it is perfect! Similarly, you will need to go with a transmission system that works efficiently, rather than sticking slavishly to a scale drive. You may even have to provide a shaft and prop system for a boat that did not have one on the full-size prototype. There are a number of examples of these.

As far as propshafts, and so on, are concerned, what you use will depend on the design of the boat. You will have to work it out for yourself, but there are a few guidelines to point you in the right direction.

For example, you may be able to use a flex shaft and strut arrangement on models of some old hydros or even on boats that were not intended to have props at all, such as jet-powered boats. On older boats such as the Ferrari hydro, you will probably need a straight solid shaft. To get the ideal shaft angle with a straight shaft, you will have to mount the motor quite a way forward in the hull. Also, do not use a universal joint (UJ) type of coupling to accommodate a shaft that is not in line with the motor shaft. High-revving motors do not like vibration, so use a solid coupling and fit the motor/mount and shaft as a single unit. If you absolutely have to use a UJ, do not use one of the plastic ones, as they are not up

Phil Davies' beautiful lifeboat, which uses brushless motors and LiPos.

Close-up of the three LiPos used: one for each motor and one for the engine sound system. The quality of the workmanship is extraordinary.

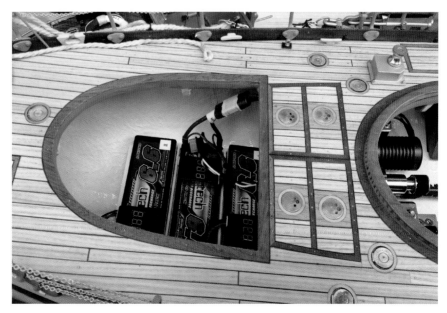

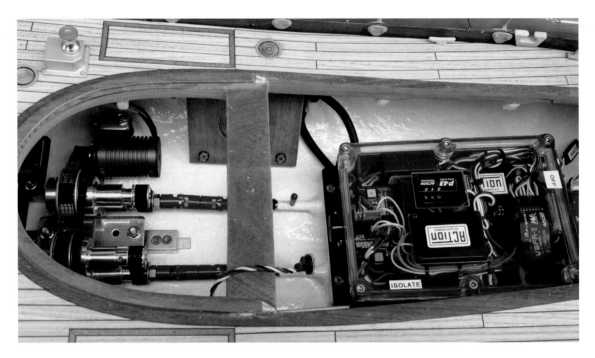

The two brushless motors in belt-drive-geared units.

to this kind of job. Use the metal ones and make sure they are lined up perfectly or they will vibrate. These metal UJs (usually stainless steel) are robust, but they can be noisy.

One solution for jet turbine-powered boats would be to use an EDF (electric-ducted fan) unit, but you would have to build a light hull as they have less thrust than a submerged or surface-drive prop and certainly less than a proper jet engine.

BATTERIES

If you are going to build a fast scale boat, because of weight and capacity advantages, it is advisable to use LiPos. Remember that they will need a proper LiPo charger, which is worth the outlay,

as most modern LiPo chargers will also charge NiCad, NiMh and even lead acid batteries. LiPos have a great power to weight ratio compared with NiMhs and NiCads. As an example, six NiMh cells of 3000 mAh capacity would give a 7.2-volt pack with a weight of 378g. A 2700 mAh LiPo pack, which gives 7.4 volts, is much smaller and weighs much less, at only 121g. In addition, the LiPo packs have a flatter discharge rate and are generally much more efficient.

Sometimes, you do need to add ballast in a model. What better way to do this than to use heavier batteries, as you obviously need them anyway? If you have purchased a decent modern charger, you will be able to charge all the battery types you might want to use.

Above all else, enjoy your boating!

Glossary

Aeration: the effect that occurs when a submerged propeller is allowed to draw air down from the surface. Usually causes partial or complete loss of thrust.

Ampere or amp: unit of electrical current. The usual way to think about electric current is to compare it to a fluid flowing in a pipe. Voltage can be considered as the pressure the fluid is under, amps or current as the quantity of fluid flowing per unit of time.

Amp-hour: unit of electrical energy capacity of a cell or battery.

Arcing: sparking or brushfire that occurs between the brushes and the commutator in a brushed motor.

Armature: the rotating part of a conventional brushed motor containing the commutator and motor windings.

Battery: term used to describe a collection of individual power cells connected together, usually in series.

Beryllium copper: soft, bronze-coloured metal used for making propellers.

Brush: part of a conventional motor that rides over the copper commutator segments to supply electrical energy to the motor windings. Brushes are usually made from carbon with varying amounts of silver and copper added, depending on the intended use of the motor.

Capacity: measure of energy storage of a cell or battery.

Cat (catamaran): twin-hulled vessel joined by a bridging section capable of generating aerodynamic lift to increase speed.

Cavitation: pockets of water vapour caused by excessive pressure drop, typically due to incorrect propeller selection.

Centre of gravity (CofG): balance point.

Centre of lift: point at which hydrodynamic or aerodynamic forces act.

Cobalt (samarium-cobalt): expensive magnetic material, exhibiting high Curie point (temperature at which a permanent magnet loses its magnetism) and high magnetic flux density (see 'Magnetic flux density').

Curie point: Temperature at which a permanent magnet loses its magnetism.

Commutator: part of a conventional motor that collects electrical energy from the brushes and passes it into the motor windings. Acts as a speed switch, switching the different segments of the armature on and off at the right time.

Deadrise angle: angle of the hull bottom from the horizontal.

Deep V: monohull with deadrise angle of 20 degrees or more.

Diode: electric device that allows current to flow in one direction only.

Direct drive: motor coupled directly to propshaft without reduction gearing.

Drag: frictional force of a fluid (air and water) moving over a surface.

Drive system: means of coupling a motor and propeller together.

'Dump': slang term for the discharging of a cell pack at the end of a run.

Efficiency: measure of how much energy is lost when converted from one form to another. For example, brushed electric motors convert about 75 per cent of the input energy into mechanical output energy, with the rest wasted as heat due to friction and resistance. Brushless motors are more efficient.

End bell: part of a motor containing the brush gear and the rear bearing.

Energy: capacity to perform useful work. Energy cannot be created or destroyed, but it can change form. Fast electric boats convert chemical energy into electrical energy, then into mechanical rotational energy then into forward kinetic energy. A certain amount of energy is lost during each conversion.

ESC: electronic speed control.

Epoxy: plastic resin used for laminating glass cloth and in two-part adhesives.

FET: (field effect transistor): solid-state semi-conductor component used to achieve efficient high-speed switching in an electronic speed controller.

Free-running speed: the rpm at which an unloaded motor will turn when a voltage is applied. Also known as 'no load speed'.

Gearbox: device using gear wheels to reduce shaft output speed and increase torque output and efficiency of electric motors.

Hollows: also known as 'hooks', depressions in the bottom of the hull that act like large trim tabs sucking the boat on to the water.

Horsepower: unit of power, now outdated. 1 horsepower is equivalent to 746 watts.

Hydrodynamic lift: lift created by the downward deflection of water off the bottom of a hull.

Hydroplane: fast racing boat that has minimal contact with the water, usually planing on only three small points.

IC: internal combustion.

ID: inside diameter.

Induction: generation of electrical current in a conductor by the changes in current of a neighbouring conductor, in this case in the windings of an electric motor. Can cause sparking between the commutator and the brushes, and is worse in motors with lots of turns of thin wire than in those with fewer turns of thicker wire.

Kilowatt: 1000 watts (*see* 'Watt').

Laminations: part of each motor pole around which the enamel-coated copper wires are wound, made from many thin silicon steel layers for electromagnetic efficiency.

LiPos: short name for lithium polymer batteries.

Magnet: The magnets in the DC motors used in FE boating are permanent magnets, made from naturally occurring materials. Cheap motors use a ferrite or iron-based magnetic material. More expensive high-performance motors may use magnets made from samarium-cobalt or neodymium-iron-boron.

Magnetic field: the invisible force field produced by a permanent magnet or when electricity is passed through a conductor. Electric motors use the field created by passing a current through the motor windings to oppose the field of the permanent magnets in the motor case to produce rpm.

Magnetic flux density: measure of the strength of a magnetic field. Expressed in the SI unit Tesla or the older unit Gauss.

Monohull: single-hulled vessel riding on one large area of contact with the water.

Neodym: neodymium-iron-boron, expensive magnet material exhibiting very high flux density, but with a lower Curie point than cobalt.

NiCad (nickel cadmium): rechargeable cell using nickel oxide hydroxide and metallic cadmium as electrodes.

NiMH (nickel metal hydride): rechargeable cell using nickel oxide hydroxide with a hydrogen-absorbing alloy for the negative electrode.

No load speed: *see* 'Free-running speed'.

OD: outside diameter.

Ohm: unit of electrical resistance.

Parallel: arrangement of the components in an electrical circuit where the positive poles are all connected together and the negative poles are all connected together so that each component 'sees' the same voltage.

PTFE: polytetrafluoroethylene, frequently known under the trade name Teflon. Used for low friction liners in shaft tubes for flexible drive shafts.

Pitch: the distance a propeller would travel forwards in each rotation assuming 100% efficiency and no slip. Usually expressed as a ratio of propeller diameter.

Planing: skimming over the water's surface, displacing little or no volume of water.

Poles: segments of the armature around which the motor windings are wound in a brushed motor.

Porpoising: vertical pitching motion due to incorrect location of the CofG, a radiused transom or curved/warped hull bottom.

Power: rate at which useful work is done. Electrical power is measured in watts (*see* 'Watt').

Propeller: device that converts rotational energy into thrust and forward motion.

Prop walk: prop walk happens when a spinning prop pushes the stern of the boat sideways. With model boats this means the boat will try to veer to the right. This effect is more prevalent with surface-drive props.

Resistance: opposition to the flow of electric current, expressed in ohms. Using the analogy of water in a pipe, whenever the flow is restricted, less water (current) will flow. Resistance wastes electrical energy as heat.

Rpm: rotational speed expressed in revolutions per minute.

Series: circuit arrangement where the components are connected one after the other so that each component receives the same amount of current.

Tend to Submarine: the tendency of a boat with the CofG too far forward to start to dive bow first rather than rising onto the plane.

Timing: position of the brush gear in a brushed electric motor relative to the magnets. Also variable settings in a brushless speed controller (ESC). Timing determines motor efficiency, rpm and current drain.

Torque: rotational force applied about a fixed centre, for example, in an electric motor.

Turns: typically, the number of times a length of wire is wound around each pole of the armature in a brushed electric motor. For example, a twelve-turn triple has three lengths of wire wound twelve times around each pole.

Volt: unit of electromotive force. Voltage is the factor that controls motor rpm. (*See* Ampere.)

Voltage drop: reduction in voltage due to resistance when current flows through a component such as a motor, speed controller, length of wire or other device that has some resistance.

Watt: measure of electrical power, equivalent to 1 joule per second. 1 watt of electrical energy is produced by supplying 1 amp at 1 volt. Watts = volts x amps or $P = VI$.

Suppliers

Component Shop (component-shop.co.uk)
LiPos, connectors, cables, etc.

Doctor Props (doctorprops.torgg.com)
High-quality propellers from a company based in Ukraine

Eco Master (ecomaster.torgg.com)
General parts for racing boats (Ukraine)

Easy Composites (easycomposites.co.uk)
Carbon fibre, resin, etc. (UK)

ETTI (etti.com.hk)
Hulls and general parts for racing boats (Hong Kong)

Hydro & Marine (hydromarine.de)
Hulls and general parts for racing boats (Germany)

Kings Lynn Model Shop (kingslynnmodelshop.co.uk)
Retail and online model shop (UK)

Leopard (leopardhobby.com)
Brushless motors (China)

Mini Mecca RC (mini-mecca-rc.com)
General parts for racing (France)

mlm Solutions (mlmsolutions.biz)
Bespoke design and engineering services (UK)

Model Fixings (modelfixings.co.uk)
Bearings, washers, screws etc. (UK)

Model Marine Supplies (modelmarinesupplies.co.uk)
Octura props and hardware

Prestwich Model Boats (prestwich.ndirect.co.uk)
General parts for racing boats (UK)

RC Bearings (rcbearings.co.uk)
Bearings and hardware (UK)

Redzone LiPos
Batteries (China)

RoaringTop LiPos (roaringtop.de)
Batteries (Europe)

Scorpion Systems (scorpionsystem.com)
Brushless motors (Hong Kong)

Simply Bearings (simplybearings.co.uk)
Bearings, lubricants and adhesives (UK)

Tenshock (tenshock.com)
General parts for racing boats (China)

TP Power Europe (tppowereurope.com) Brushless motors, propellers and more (German warehouse)

WheelSpin Models (wheelspinmodels.co.uk)
General model parts (UK)

Index